TRANSFORMING WORDS

TRANSFORMING WORDS

Six Essays on Preaching

Edited and with an Introduction by
WILLIAM F. SCHULZ

Skinner House: Boston

Copyright © 1984 Unitarian Universalist Association

A Skinner House book published under the
auspices of the Unitarian Universalist Association

Printed in the United States of America

ISBN #0-933840-22-5

500   4/84   1978
7902-000

Cover design by J. Hempstead

Note: The Unitarian Universalist Association is com-
mitted to using gender-inclusive language in all of
its publications. In this volume, *quoted material*
which is gender-exclusive is identified with the Latin
word *sic*—meaning "thus," as in "thus in the
original"—following the first such usage in a passage. In this way the reader is alerted to the presence of a gender-exclusive usage while the literary
integrity of the original is retained.

TO LINDALU

Who has listened to them all,
sometimes again and again.

CONTENTS

INTRODUCTION

I

Unitarian Universalists display a kind of splendid ambivalence about preaching. On the one hand, emerging as we did from the Protestant Reformation, we know that religion requires articulation — not just incense and not just chanting, evocative as those and other rituals may be of religious experience. We believe, this is to say, in theology.

And yet, emerging as we did from the *left wing* of the Reformation, we also affirm idiosyncratic articulation, popularly heralded as the priesthood of all believers. That, after all, is what the left wing of the Reformation was all about: a stodgy uniformity would never do; God was just too grand to be manifested only through a Calvin, much less a priest. The Holy Spirit, our forebears said, speaks through many tongues, including lay ones. (The only caveat was that the Holy Spirit not speak gibberish but use a language others understood.) We believe, this is to say, in dialectical (read "argumentative") theology.*

This presents something of a dilemma for our professional religious leaders — particularly when the areas of the preachers' expertise, once clearly denoted as the Bible and the Church Tradition, have either been eroded or diluted in importance by culture's desacralizing stream. Some preachers, it's true, will try to reassert the authority of a Biblical or churchly knowledge while others will abandon that altogether in favor of a kind of intellectual mélange, a bit of this and a bit of that, with no one flavor dominating. In some cases and some settings, of course, one of these two strategies may work but most of the time, I suspect, they fail, the first because it is too narrow and the second because it is too wide. The second, in particular, is doomed because, after all, every layperson also has the

*The dilemma of idiosyncratic articulation (and its corresponding diminishment of doctrinal identity) was evident from what Earl Morse Wilbur in his *History of Unitarianism* identifies as only the second organized gathering of Unitarians in history when, on Christmas Day, 1559, forty-seven ministers and fourteen laypeople gathered in Wegrow, Poland and, unable to reach agreement on infant baptism, agreed instead "that since in matters of faith no one . . . may lord it over another, nor be forced, each should enjoy freedom of conscience," this despite the fact that only eight of the sixty-one gathered continued to favor infant baptism.[1]

recipe for "mélange" and some know considerably more about its ingredients than ministers.

What is required therefore, is to re-discover and proclaim the particular calling of as preacher. The sermon is, we must admit, a most peculiar vehicle for the advancement of a proposition — "twenty minutes," Henry Ward Beecher called it, "to wake the dead" and twenty minutes (or even thirty) is too short to explore a subject thoroughly and too long to keep a preacher's ignorance under wraps. "What shall we preach our first sermon on?" a graduating student at Union Theological Seminary once asked Reinhold Niebuhr. "Fred," Niebuhr replied, "when I began my ministry in a church, my problem was not to preach about on the first Sunday but on the second after I'd preached everything I knew on the first."[2]

Could it be, though, that a sermon is not *primarily* an intellectual exercise? It surely is that in part but perhaps not entirely or primarily. This is, I believe, an assumption shared by all six of our essayists. But if a sermon is not primarily an intellectual exercise, what is it? That is the burden of this collection.

And it is a burden precisely because, I suggest, whether our faith will be renewed will be in large part dependent upon whether we stop apologizing for our preaching and whether we stop preaching in such a way that demands apology. Unitarian Universalism, for good or ill, is stuck with preaching as the principal mode for the conveyance of our Good News. In light of that, we had better take it very, very seriously, improve it as we need, and promote it as we can.

The event for which five out of these six essays were prepared signaled the recognition by the Unitarian Universalist Association and its related theological schools of the crucial role of preaching in the religious transaction and, moreover, that preaching can be *taught*. With funding provided by the Liberal Religious Charitable Society and accommodations arranged by Meadville/Lombard Theological School,* more than twenty practicing ministers and thirty theological students met for five days in August, 1982, in Chicago, in the company of five of our six essayists. (Roy Phillips' contribution to this volume was delivered in April, 1980, to a Con-

---

*Particular appreciation needs to be expressed to Gene Reeves, Meadville/Lombard's Dean, and Randy Vaughan, the School's Business Manager.

vocation on Worship sponsored by the Unitarian Universalist Ministers Association and the Liberal Religious Education Directors Association in Newport, Rhode Island; originally published in *Kairos* [Number 19, Summer 1980, pp. 10-12], the essay's excellence prompted its inclusion here.)

The participants in the five-day preaching seminar did not just listen to these lectures, however. Each participant met daily in a small practicum group with eight to ten colleagues and an essayist, there to deliver in the course of the seminar two sermons for critique. Videotape work was available; chapels were presented twice daily (including one chapel by each of the essayists who thereby had to "practice what they lectured"); and evening panels addressed the "tricks" of the preaching trade (filing systems, styles of preparation, etc.), the relationship between preaching and liturgy and the "preacher's persona," this last a rather fluid topic which had been intended to illuminate such issues as how to deal with criticism from a congregation and what differences there may be, if any, between the preaching styles, subjects, and attitudes of men and women. (Whether because it came on the last night of the seminar or because the topic was too diffuse or, on the contrary, too emotionally charged, this last session was the least successful and its second question — that of gender differences in preaching — remains, unfortunately, relatively unexplored.[3]) Evaulations of the seminar as a whole as well as the fact that more than thirty people who wished to participate had to be turned away (thrity people, despite the meager travel subsidies available!) convince me that occasions such as this ought to be far less rare; ought, indeed, to be a regular feature of our continuing education programs and the preparation of our students for ministry.

And a personal reaction to the seminar: I had begun the week expecting to hear a goodly share of abysmal offerings. I ended it mightly impressed by the preachers who stood before me, the fitness of their words and the passion of their testimony. There is such a thing, I can attest, as a "preacher's high," born of clarity and conviction, distilled in a *kairotic* moment, and this I had witnessed time and time again. There was little to apologize for here. Instead, I caught a glimmer of what a religious movement which truly prizes preaching could become.

II

Good preaching is always marked by tension, the tension, for example, between the linear and the affective. Roy Phillips elucidates this matter in the second essay of this volume but, as Roy well recognizes, he is far from the first to struggle with it. In his sermon entitled "Preaching Christ," delivered at the ordination of the Rev. John Emery Abbot in 1815, William Ellery Channing advised that, though the "rational method of preaching Christianity is important," Christianity should also "be so preached as to interest the affections, to awaken contrition and fear, veneration and love . . ."

> Some preachers [he went on to say], from observing the pernicious effects of violent . . . appeals to the passions, have fallen into the opposite error . . . , have addressed men (*sic*) as mere creatures of intellect; they have forgotten that affection is as essential to our nature as thought . . . , that the union of reason and sensibility is the health of the soul . . . They have preached ingeniously and the hearer has pronounced the teaching true. But the truth, coldly imparted and coldly received, has been forgotten as fast as heard . . . The sun warms at the same moment that is enlightens and, unless religious truth be addressed at once to the reason and the affections . . . , it is a useless splendor . . .[4]

Here is Channing emphasizing the power of fervor, sentiment, and metaphor.

But twenty-five years later, in his Charge at the ordination of the Rev. John S. Dwight, the tone is considerably different. When preaching Christian truth, Channing urged Dwight, "communicate it with all possible plainness and simplicity."

> Do not [he continued] . . . overlay it with ornaments or false colors to make it more effectual . . . Be willing to disappoint your hearers . . . , to seem cold, rather than to "o'erstep the modesty" of truth . . . Do not, to be striking, dress up the truth in paradoxes . . . I would caution you . . . against straining for effect, against efforts to startle or dazzle the hearer . . . Prefer the true to the dazzling . . . Trust is the power which is to

conquer the world and you cannot toil too much to give clear perceptions of it.[5]

The two Channings are not, of course, at odds — they can well be reconciled — but the tension is apparent.

If, as the theologian Sallie McFague says,

> Metaphor . . . is *the* way of human knowledge. It is not simply the way we can embellish something we can know in some other way. There is no other way,[6]

and if good preaching (perhaps, indeed, good religion) is largely metaphorical, then nonetheless we must be careful that our penchant for the metaphorical, so powerful and so charming, not "o'erstrp the modesty of truth," not slip into the mawkish, not make impossible the jeremiad, not give sanction to the vacuous, not encourage a preacher's hiding.

A preacher's hiding — now there is a second common tension of the art. "There was never a philosopher," Shakespeare says in *Much Ado About Nothing*, "that could endure the toothache patiently."[7] How intricate is the relationship between a preacher's words and that preacher's life. This is the labyrinth which my own chapter wants, albeit fails, to untangle. Perhaps the Rev. Virginia Knowles, one of the participants in our seminar, offered as good a text for it as any: "I once knew a preacher," she says, "whose sermons seemed to be affecting my life more than his own!"

Or consider the tension of prophecy, that between justice and mercy, forgiveness and righteousness. In her portraits of *Universalist and Unitarian Women Ministers*, Catherine Hitchings quotes the description of the Rev. Frances E. Cheney's sermons as reflecting her "literary turn of mind," sermons "beautiful and restful and filled with that spiritual power that makes human life . . . happier."[8] But of the Rev. Catherine Matteson Hughes it was said that she was a "strong, clear preacher [who] had an intense passion to see her theology applied to the actual conditions around her . . . on equal suffrage and temperance . . . ."[9] Is the difference no more than a matter of temperament or does it strike at the very core of the religious enterprise? (It can surely strike at the very heart of the religious pocketbook.)

To hear Theodore Parker, naturally, there is no question:

> You [a congregation] may hire your servants to preach as you bid, to spare your vices and flatter your follies, to prophesy smooth things and say, "It is peace" when there is no peace. Yet in so doing you weaken and enthral yourselves. And alas for that man (*sic*) who consents to think one thing in his closet and preach another in his pulpit! God shall judge him in his mercy, not man in his wrath. But over his study and over his pulpit might be writ, "EMPTINESS;" and on his canonical robes, on his forehead and right hand, "DECEIT, DECEIT."[10]

But Judith Hoehler, who addresses this issue for us in a manner both scholarly and personal, sees the prophetic dimension in its full complexity.

And there are other issues, equally important. David Rankin wrestles with the elementary question of authority, ever thorny, ever fiercesome, but so basic that we can hardly wander far without its haunting us again. And Joyce Smith assures us that our preaching really *does* matter if by "matter" we mean that it changes people's lives. Preaching is, after all, but one portion of the minister's responsibility and it is urgent that we know that the good preacher is, in the very act of speaking, attending too to the call as pastor. Finally, for an historical perspective, Irving Murray offers a survey of our preaching, both past and present, and not just "ours" but the American nation's too.

III

What we have here, then, is at least a prolegomenon to a practical theology of preaching. I am told that Alan Watts, the late Eastern guru of Western theology, once explained his departure from the church this way: "It was not that the church didn't practice what it preached" he said, ". . . but that it preached." Well, if the very act of preaching was enough to drive Watts out of the church, imagine how much more speedily he would take his leave in the face of a book *about* preaching . . . and by six preachers at that! For us who stay in the church, however — and especially for us who try to preach in it — I trust that these lectures will have some utility.

I have called the book *Transforming Words* and I mean that in two senses. First, I mean "transforming" as a verb to describe what preachers do when they take words up into a sermon, transforming them from the vernacular into the service of the holy. If a sermon is in any way an art unto itself, then the self-same words, when spoken in sermonic context in the larger body of a service, take on a meaning and a texture different from their pronouncement anywhere else.

And because I believe those sermonic words to be not only different from but *richer than* their pronouncement anywhere else, I mean "transforming" also as an adjective to describe what makes them richer, what kind of words they are, namely, words which change the speaker, the hearer, and the very world itself. Words in this shape embody what Frederick Buechner calls "the great power that language has to move and in some measure to transform the human heart."[11]

Shortly before his death, Theodore Parker wrote to his beloved congregation of his "Experience as a Minister." "To compose sermons and preach them to multitudes . . .," he said, "this has been my great delight."

> My life is in [those sermons] and all my character, its good and ill; thereby you know me better than I, perhaps, myself — for a man's (sic) words and his face when excited in sermon and prayer tell all he is, the reflection of what he has done . . . Sermons are never out of my mind . . . [They] come . . . spontaneously by night and give themselves to me and even in my sleep say they are meant for you.[12]

For us preachers, the words and the models which are our lives are almost the only tools we have, the only tools with which to meet the mortal and the monstrous. This means that we must trust the words and hone them well and treat them as a treasure. For Paul's questions to the Romans are well put to us: "How shall they hear without a preacher?" and "How shall they preach except that they be sent?"[13] And the answer is, "They shall hear poorly," but the other answer is, "Ah, yes, but listen, friends, we have been sent!"

William F. Schulz

FROM THE MASTHEAD
TO THE HATCHES:
The Sources of Authority in the
Liberal Pulpit

David O. Rankin

When I stood in the pulpit of the Seamen's Bethel in New Bedford, Massachusetts, I was aware of a fictional predecessor. Herman Melville had created a preacher of immense proportion. In the opening pages of *Moby Dick*, the people gathered in the Bethel for the blessing of the fleet:

> Father Mapple rose, and in the mild voice of unassuming author-ity, ordered the scattered people to condense. 'Starboard gangway, there! Side away to larboard-larboard gangway to starboard! Midships! Midships! There was a low rumbling of heavy sea-boots among the benches, and a still slighter shuffling of women's shoes, and all was quiet again, and every eye on the preacher. He paused a little; folded his large hands across his chest; uplifted his closed eyes; and offered a prayer so deeply devout that he seemed kneeling and praying at the bottom of the sea.[1]

So I, too, stood in the pulpit, which is shaped like the prow of a ship and extends out over the pews, and I thought of my colleagues who sent sailors into the mystery of the sea.

I have spoken in many distinguished pulpits of America. The oldest is the First Unitarian Church of Watertown, Massachusetts. It was the second church organized on the soil of New England. It was the first to assert and apply the principle of Congregational Independence.[2] George Washington and Thomas Jefferson both graced the pulpit.

The highest is King's Chapel of Boston, Massachusetts. In an Anglican setting, a winding stairway leads almost to the ceiling where the preacher peers down on the heads of the congregation. In the heat of the summer, it is not clear whether one is standing on the throne of heaven or in the fires of hell.

The safest is the First Unitarian Church of Providence, Rhode Island. A special key opens a secret door in the side that leads to a series of steps which end at the top of the pulpit almost twenty feet above the congregation. The preacher can only be reached by large artillery.

The most notable is the First Unitarian Church of San Francisco, California. Emerson and Longfellow, Alan Watts and the Beat

Generation, Margaret Sanger and Norman Cousins, Susan Anthony pulpit has supported them all. (I am sure you have your own list which is equally distinguished.)

But whether I speak in the historic meetinghouses of New England or in the magnificent cathedrals of the West or in the rural frame buildings of Georgia and Minnesota or in the rich adornments of Tulsa and Manhattan, there is always the identical feeling: I am so afraid!

I remember one of my first experiences in a pulpit. I was very nervous. The pulpit was too short for my body. The sound system was buzzing and ringing. The congregation was large and unfamiliar. And when I delivered the line, "Do you know that there are people in the 20th Century who believe in devils, demons, exorcism?", three candles fell from the wall to the floor! I saved the day by asking if there was a priest in the house.

Yet these are the normal fears and anxieties of the pulpit. The trembling hands, the knocking knees, and the stomach on the verge of eruption are common to all public speakers, even to athletes and entertainers. But they feel justified in their performance by a natural talent or an intellectual ability. The fear of the preacher is much more profound. The anxiety is never ending. It is a permanent condition of the soul.

Of course, I have known preachers who are not afraid. They are scholars, lecturers, toastmasters, or jolly good friends of the congregation who define their preaching in a secular manner and assess their effectiveness on the basis of the roles they have chosen. Usually they are shallow and frivolous professionals, like Andrew Mackeral in *The Mackeral Plaza*, an urbane intellectual who resigns from the ministry when he discovers that God *does* answer prayers.[3]

For the serious preacher, however, the pulpit has dimensions that are scary and threatening. It was Dean Samuel Miller of Harvard Divinity School who wrote: "Anyone who steps into this kind of pulpit, into this prow where the storm strikes first and the dark is thickest, knows right well the terror of the position."[4] But before I explore the major source of terror, I will briefly list some other contributing factors. They relate to the special burden of the masthead.

The Pulpit as a Symbol

First, the pulpit is a symbol of freedom. Four hundred years ago the liberal religionists of Poland and Transylvania raised the banner of religious freedom. Their ministers were imprisoned; their churches were burned; and many were banished from their home-lands.

Three hundred years ago, the liberal churches of the American colonies asserted their independence from government control. They would choose their own ministers for their own pulpits who would not be intimidated. In the years to follow, the pulpit became the model for other freedoms in America (of speech, of the press, of assembly) as they originated in the successful experience of liberal religion. Even today, it is probably the freest space in the world, guaranteed by law and tradition to brook no censorship, harass-ment, or interruptions. It is a symbol of freedom and that is a heavy burden.

Second, the pulpit is a symbol of personality. Each preacher is a mixture: soft-hard, passive-aggressive, serious-humorous, biting-consoling, and every one is different from another. The appeal is also different. But the pulpit demands the essential truth of the individual. It will not abide for long the objectivity of the essay, the abstraction of the lecture, the remoteness of the dissertation. It requires rather a vulnerable, subjective truth which is not often expressed in our society. It is more of a confession than a speech, as each preacher is saying, "Here I am! I can be no other!" It is a symbol of personality and that is a heavy burden.

Third, the pulpit is a symbol of intimacy. If the preacher is free to confess, then all feelings, opinions, and convictions are appropriate in the pulpit. Those who attend regularly might know the preacher better than their husband or wife or even their mother and father.

But the people in the hatches are also known. In meetings, counseling, and social occasions, the preacher taps the souls of James and Sandra, Harry and Marjorie, Jane and Daniel, noting their joy as well as their pain. And out of the knowledge of each other, preacher and congregant, something happens between the pew and the pulpit which does not occur between strangers. In probing the deepest levels of faith and desire, the communication is both vivid

5

and discreet. The pulpit is a symbol of intimacy and that is a heavy burden.

Fourth, the pulpit is a symbol of prophecy. While there is always a need for variety in worship, for music, dance, drama; for prayer, singing, fellowship, only the pulpit provides the element of prophecy. For only the spoken word, from the depths of freedom, personality, and intimacy, can convey the biting edge of criticism. If the other elements of worship soothe the sensibility, it is through preaching that the hard, the hated, and the unspeakable are heard. Thus no preacher should ever seek comfort in a pulpit. No minister should ever plan for security of employment. None should ever fall in love with a particular institution. It destroys the biting edge. "I will say what I will say" must never be compromised. The pulpit is a symbol of prophecy and that is a heavy burden.

Yet the weight is increased by a final burden, the ground for all others. What right do I have to exercise freedom? What truth do I have to strain through personality? What responsibility do I have to engage in intimacy? What power do I have to utter prophecy? In short, what is the source of my authority in the pulpit? When I approach the masthead on Sunday morning, that is the question which turns the tongue to dust.

At such a moment a verbal facility and a polished style are weak companions, cosmetic devices that hide the quivering lip but do nothing for the pounding heart. The faces in the hatches are filled with hope and expectancy: "Who am I," they ask. "Is there a God?" "Can I trust the universe?" "Where do I come from?" "Where am I going?" "How shall I live?" "How can I confront the finalities of suffering and death?" And I, the minister, stand in the spotlight. Am I merely a bundle of pretensions or do I speak from a position of authority? From what source is that authority derived?

A Review of Religious Authority

Since the issue is controverial (the root cause of wars, schisms, inquisitions), a short review of religious authority might be useful. Admittedly, I embrace a Christian perspective. But liberal religion in the Western world is a product of the Judeo-Christian tradition and preaching is unique to Christianity in terms of its importance to the worship experience. Even the most ardent humanist, therefore, when leaning on a pulpit, has a debt to the past.

In the days of Jesus, there were no marble or wooden pulpits. Yet Jesus did speak in the fields and market places and organized the disciples to spread the spoken word. In the fashion of a prophet, Jesus believed that God had seized him and had filled him with the Holy Spirit. When asked by the elders and priests to describe the source of his authority, he compared himself to John the Baptist, who had been anointed by God.[5]

For Jesus, then, the traditional authorities of Jewish society were secondary, applicable only when converging with the prophecy of the Kingdom. He seldom argued. Instead, he announced! Furthermore, since it was God's word which he was announcing, all opposition to the message was a flat disobedience to the God who was speaking through him.[6] Such a notion of authority, while intense and powerful, often leads to an early death.

If Jesus could say with confidence, "It has been said by those of old, but I say unto you,"[7] the authority of James and Peter in Jerusalem was founded on a different ground. After the crucifixion the disciples returned to the synagogue to speak about their fallen leader. In effect they were a Christian sect within the Jewish community, people who believed that Jesus was the promised Messiah, that the end of the world was at hand. Their authority was derived from association. They had walked and talked with Jesus. They had received their appointments from the Son of Man. They had witnessed the miracle of the resurrection. Peter, especially, who had seemed to have been the favorite of Jesus, had a singular power in early Christianity. When he spoke in the synagogues of Israel and Asia Minor, the words were a testimony to a personal relationship.

But the next generation of Christians could not appeal to first-hand knowledge. The authority of Paul, for example, was based on a vision of the risen Lord. In the Book of Acts, Jesus appears in the vision to say of Paul, "He is a chosen vessel unto me, to bear my name before the Gentiles and Kings and the children of Israel."[8] Having no knowledge of Jesus in the flesh, Paul relied on the inner

Savior. It was Christ, himself, who had chosen him to convert the world.

Yet Paul turned to other authorities as well. Not only to the authority of Greek speculation and the genius of his own mind but also to the authority of organization, of doctrinal conformity, and of sacred writings. In the end he could stand in any of the churches he had founded and say with confidence, "If any man preacheth unto you any gospel other than that which ye received, let him be anathema."[9]

Following the death of Paul, the issue of authority was a central concern of Christianity. I will not trace the many disputes between faith and reason, scripture and philosophy, bishops, and councils, or the continuous debates over the right of ordination, the administration of the sacraments, and the line of apostolic succession. In time the scriptures were canonized; the Bishop of Rome gained ascendency; church councils in Nicea and Chalcedon forged doctrinal orthodoxy. But the haunting question still remained, "What is the source of authority?"

In *The Gnostic Gospels*, Elaine Pagels describes one such struggle. It involved the Gnostic belief that the true source of authority was "the depth of all being," the spirit of God transmitted directly to the faithful individual.[10] It was nothing less than a theological justification for disobeying the priests and bishops. Much later, George Fox would also appeal to the "inner light" in order to denounce the whole structure of Puritan authority. The mystics and visionaries, emulating the claim of Jesus, have always been troublesome.

Yet the challenges to the orthodox formula were seldom successful. From Origen and Pelagius to Huss and Wyclif, through a thousand years of bitter conflict, the hierarchial church continued to expand. It reached a peak in the thirteenth century under Pope Innocent III. In the words of Roland Bainton, "No monarch in Europe was so powerful . . . With spiritual weapons alone he held sway from Gibraltar to Jerusalem, from Stockholm to Constantinople, as the vice-regent of Christ and shepherd of the faithful."[11] Not since Jesus and Paul was the locus of authority so clearly defined. The source was Rome, traced back to Peter, the Rock.

If we returned to the Medieval Period, to look at the interior design of religious institutions, we would find no pulpits. The churches of the time were much like the Roman Catholic churches of today. The pews were the most numerous objects in the sanctuary, demanding the most space, but not in a position of prominence. The altar rail separated the congregation from the chancel, sharply defining the differing roles of the priests and the people. The chancel was the stage for the ceremony of worship, reserved for the representatives of God and framed with the glow of candles. The altar was in the center of the chancel. Here the mass was celebrated. Here the bread and wine was transformed into the flesh and blood of Christ. It was here that God resided. Looking more closely at the Medieval Church, we would see a small lectern in the wings of the chancel. Dimly lit, barely visible to the vast majority of the worshippers, it was used for the reading of the scriptures. But out of little lecterns large pulpits would grow!

When the Protestant Reformation erupted at the beginning of the 16th century, the interior design of the churches was dramatically changed. The stakes were more than architecture. In Germany Luther believed that the discourse on scripture was central to the faith so he reduced the area of the chancel, increased the size of the lectern, and brought the pulpit into a position of prominence. In Geneva Calvin believed that the sermon was a significant element of worship so he moved the pulpit to the center of the chancel, raised it high above the altar, and bathed it in the glow of candles. In terms of design, the pulpit had replaced the altar. In terms of worship, the sermon had replaced the mass. In terms of symbols, the Word of God had replaced the Body of God.

Luther understood that the function of preaching was inevitably linked to the question of authority. Though all males were priests, each with a gift and a responsibility, the preacher had a special duty to perform. Luther wrote, "The duty of a priest is to preach and, if he does not preach, he is as much a priest as a picture of a man is a man . . . It is the ministry of the Word that makes the priest and the bishop."[12] Luther opposed the authority of the popes, the councils, and the traditions of the Church by appealing to the authority of the Holy Book. If salvation was faith alone, it had to be informed by the Word of God. A minister, chosen by a congregation, was the teacher of the Word.

The floodgates had been opened. When Luther was forced by the Diet of Worms to respond to the question of his own authority, he replied, "Unless I am convicted by scripture and plain reason, I do not accept the authority of popes and councils; my conscience is captive to the Word of God . . . the Christian must examine and judge for himself."[13] Unwittingly, without fully realizing the extent of those remarks, Luther had introduced the justification for Protestant individualism. Words like "reason," "conscience," and "judge," would bring an end to the Medieval Period.

The Left-Wing of the Reformation produced a startling variety of responses to the question of authority. For example, Sebastian Franck, a mystic, argued that the Word of God is an emanation, an essence, an outpouring, which is available to all people everywhere.[14] Guillaume Postel, a universalist, aspired to unite the major religions of the world into a single church and an ultimate harmony.[15] Michael Servetus, a rationalist, yearned for a compatibility between late Scholastic philosophy and the teachings of Christianity.[16] By and large, the Left-Wing relied on the Bible as the ultimate source of authority. But once the scriptures were open to individual interpretation, the worst fears of orthodoxy had been realized. The authorities of organization and tradition were secondary.

A modern approach was provided by Sebastian Castellio, influenced by the humanism of the Enlightenment. He was an Italian professor of Greek in Geneva during the reign of Calvin. In a book On the Art of Doubting and of Knowing, he set forth three sources for religious knowledge: experience, revelation, and reason. While all are important, the first two are subject to the third for clarification and elaboration.[17]

But Castellio went even further on behalf of individual freedom. After establishing the difference between faith and knowledge and attacking both the Romans and the Reformers, he affirmed the right to heresy itself: "To seek truth and to utter what one believes to be true can never be a crime. No one must be forced to accept a conviction. Conviction is free."[18]

Yet the question was far from settled. What is experience, revelation, or reason? How are they blended and balanced in a particular situation? Is the preacher entirely free to express a personal conviction? The centuries passed in controversy.

It is interesting, if not humorous, to note that the liberal tradition offers no authority to speak on authority. The threads of a coherent doctrine are hanging out all over. While Channing made a valiant effort to balance rationality, moral experience, and Christian revelation into a general theory of authority, he left no permanent legacy.[19] While Emerson adopted the Over-Soul as the source of moral sentiment and the revealer of truth to the individual (a continuous, democratic revelation), he did not deal with institutional authority.[20] While Parker resolved "to preach nothing as religion that I have not experienced inwardly and made my own,"[21] he never developed a position on the subjectivity of religious knowledge. Not unrelated to the issue of authority is the fact that Channing was forced out of his own pulpit, that Emerson resigned from the ministry under fire, and that Parker was shunned by most Unitarians. It is a sober reflection for those of us who are less than giants!

I suggest, however, that the liberal theory of authority from the Reformation to the present day is lacking not in the essential contents, but in the coherence of the parts to the whole. For example, I know a preacher in New England who relies heavily on a Doctrine of the Church — its ritual, tradition, and congregational polity — but he gives little credence to personal experience and the moral imperative to engage the world. I know a preacher in the West who appeals to reason and philosophy, to prophecy and social action, but he has little regard for the revelations of faith or the requirement of tradition in a religious community. Similar patterns are repeated over and over again. Our pulpits are filled with men and women who stand on one leg or on no legs at all. It is neither wise nor necessary. A liberal theory of authority can be described.

The Sources of Liberal Authority

First, there is the academic authority of the pulpit. Though it is often forgotten, all ministers are certified by an educational process which is long, arduous, and expensive. In keeping with the principle of an educated clergy, the psychologists and professors have given their stamp of approval. Indeed, in terms of a formal education, the standard of excellence required of a liberal preacher is as high as that of the Rabbi and the Jesuit. This is a source of strength on Sunday morning.

Second, there is the denominational authority of the pulpit. Though the process is sometimes irritating, all ministers are reviewed by the Unitarian Universalist Association's Office of Ministry and the Ministerial Fellowship Committee. Forms, interviews, and sermons are all used to evaluate the intelligence, personality, and loyalty of the candidate. There are probably more people involved in the judging of a liberal minister than in any other denomination. This is a source of strength on Sunday morning.

Third, there is the authority of tradition in the pulpit. Though this is easily ignored, all ministers are imbued with a religious tradition which provides a framework and a perspective for communication. It is not mere history. The liberal preacher walks and talks with the heroes and heroines of the faith; lives and breathes in the atmosphere of freedom and toleration; and molds the spoken word with the ideas, models, and principles of a rich tradition. It is a source of strength on Sunday morning.

Fourth, there is the authority of community in the pulpit. Though this authority is taken for granted, all ministers are ordained and installed by a particular congregation. Much of the power of the pulpit flows from the contractual relationship between the minister and the people. The liberal preacher, chosen by the community, has the right and the obligation to speak the Word. For the laying on of hands is a sacred ceremony, where authority is passed from the hatches to the masthead. And this too is a source of strength on Sunday morning.

Finally, there is the authority of a personal faith. While the authorities of education, denomination, tradition, and community are extremely significant, the liberal preacher must also be called to the pulpit by a deep personal conviction which yearns to be expressed to the world. It is a seizure of the spirit, a captivity of the soul, a profound moral earnestness which not only compels the preacher to mount the pulpit but also comforts and sustains in the midst of the storm.

In my own experience the ground of faith is most important. The belief in a creative and loving God; the belief in the incarnation of

Jesus Christ; the belief in the healing power of prayer; the belief in salvation by grace and action; the belief in the victory of goodness over evil; the belief in the mysteries and revelations of existence which continually unfold — all of these represent an authority wrenched from life and tested by reason. And they are sources of strength on Sunday morning.

The content of faith will vary in the liberal pulpit but the process of selection is always the same. Hans Küng has written:

> I see, know, and judge in the light of what I am myself, in my whole concrete existence: placed in a quite definite situation, consciously or unconsciously dependent on certain values and experiences, involved in one set of social conditions or another, and characterized by personal interests . . . In the light of my subjectivity, the direction of my perception and imagination continually determines the selection of what in fact is perceived or even remembered. I myself give color and emphasis to reality.[22]

In other words, I make my truth . . . I decide . . . I push on.

I do not imply that faith should be reduced to a subjectivist individualism, for I have already argued that the preacher is constantly informed by education, denomination, tradition, community, and other encounters with the world. In the end, however, a liberal theory of authority must rely on personal decision — not only for the specific content of faith, but also for the acceptance of the other authorities as well.

In fact, I dare submit that all theories of authority rest ultimately on personal decision. When Jesus appeals to God, when Paul appeals to the risen Christ, when Luther appeals to Scripture, when Emerson appeals to the Over-Soul, they are defining the end-result of their religious odyssey. Along the way, however, each appeal to a religious authority is the product of a multitude of personal choices and decisions based on those life experiences found to be the most meaningful. So the arrow points back to the individual — whether liberal, orthodox, or evangelical. Truth is a series of choices made in time.

Küng describes the core of authority with an analogy to the "heart," of which the bodily organ is only a symbol: "It is the

13

personal, spiritual core of the individual, the innermost operative center, the starting point of dynamic relationships, the precision instrument for grasping reality in its wholeness."[23] It is not a "thing." Neither is it pure reason or wild emotion. It is the spontaneously present, intuitively sensing, existentially apprehending, totally opening, and, in the widest sense, the sorting and selecting of the data of existence. Preaching is the serving of pieces of the heart — baked in the spices of selected authority.

Before leaving the Seamen's Bethel, I thought again of Father Mapple. He, too, had stood in the pulpit with the authority of a fine education, with the authority of denominational approval, with the authority of rich tradition, with the authority of a religious community, and with the authority of a personal faith. Yet after delivering the sermon, he dropped to his knees. "He said no more, but, slowly waving a benediction, covered his face with his hands, and so remained kneeling, till all the people had departed, and he was left alone in the place."[24] It is a striking posture, and one I have often repeated, if only in the chambers of the mind. For just as the ancient altar required the act of kneeling, so, too, does the modern pulpit demand an act of penance and humility. The speaking of the Word is a perilous undertaking, calling forth the deepest expression of sincerity and genuineness, but fear is the beginning of wisdom.

PREACHING AS A
SACRAMENTAL EVENT

Roy D. Phillips

I speak in support of preaching. I speak for it as a potentially most powerful and most creative religious transaction. I affirm its centrality in the total task of the ministry. I assert its necessity to a worshipping congregation for the continual vitalizing of its liturgical life. I speak of preaching, not as an addendum to worship, but as itself an act of worship, as an integral element of the liturgy. I speak of preaching as a sacramental event.

This endorsement of preaching, however, is not without reservation. Neither is it made out of ignorance of the widespread ramshackle state of the craft in our day. Nor is it unmindful of the fact that preaching is not highly regarded in this culture at this time.

There was a time when in some communities the preacher's message was thought significant enough to be reported in summary form in Monday evening's newspaper. Today books, plays, films, television shows and musical recordings are considered important enough to merit critical review but sermons are largely ignored by the culture as a whole.

Even in the churches, where one might expect to find preaching highly valued, the sentiment about preachers and sermons is often indifference, when not downright disapproval. In the judgment of many in the mainline churches, the best sermon is the briefest one. In liberal congregations there may be no sermon at all and, often, if there is one and if it is something a listener finds worthwhile, then some other name is sought for it. It is called a "talk" or a "pulpit essay" or a "pulpit address" for fear that calling it "sermon" might offend the speaker or might insult the intelligence of any astute, attentive listener.

Perhaps the best indicator of our age's response to the sermon is found in certain prevalent idiomatic expressions heard in circles beyond the churches:

"Not another one of your sermons!"

"Too preachy!"

"Don't you preach to me!"

These exclamations contain within them elements of the pre-reflective sentiment of many in our time toward preaching: that it is a verbose or sanctimonious or moralistic undertaking; that it is authoritarian or remote or that it is all of these.

I am not so presumptuous as to suppose that an essay of mine could change the mind of the times about the nature and the value of preaching. This is not my concern. The sentiment of the age regarding the art and the craft of preaching should serve, rather, as a signal to preachers that something is dreadfully amiss. When the primary public activity of those who see themselves as helpers, as ministers to the world, is so drastically devalued by the world, then some effort to alter the situation should be vigorously sought.

Some among us would advocate that we accept the world's opinion and preach less or preach not at all. Some would have us either radically alter the nature of our preaching or camouflage the preaching we do so it appears to be something else. Some might advise us to ignore the world's opinion and to continue doing just what we have always done.

My suggestion, however, is that we heighten our consciousness regarding what we are doing in our sermons, that we examine carefully our present conceptualizations about preaching and that we seek to replace inadequate conceptualizations with a more carefully thought-through understanding — theological understanding — of the nature and function of preaching. This essay strives toward such a new, more conscious, more articulate theological conceptualization of preaching. It seeks to introduce among us the conviction that preaching is most powerfully creative when it is viewed as a sacramental event.

Models for Preaching[1]

It appears not to be widely noticed by preachers or by laypersons that there float among us numerous pre-reflective understandings of what preaching is and what it seeks to accomplish. These internal, underlying understandings significantly determine what preachers can do when they stand in their pulpits. They affect what members of congregations can hear when preachers preach. Implicit understandings of what preachers do probably also predispose many persons to keep themselves far from churches, or, if they ever do come near, to stop their ears from really hearing anything of importance to their lives.

I believe it will be helpful for us to recognize the existence among us of these implicit models of preaching. Such recognition may help us to increase our effectiveness in the pulpit but, at the least, it will help us to gain better understanding of why we are sometimes ineffective with certain individuals or groups. It may be that our model of preaching and their models may be quite different, so that what we believe we are sending out to them may be significantly different from what they are able to receive.

I will specify eight models of preaching which are prevalent today within the popular and the professional mind. Largely derived from activities in the culture outside the church, seldom made articulate or even consciously entertained, these models provide the implicit criteria by which particular sermons are prepared and by which they are criticized or praised.

Probably the most prevalent model for preaching within the liberal churches is that of the *college professor lecturing to a class of students*. One person who presumably has special knowledge stands before a group of people who presumably lack that knowledge and speaks to them in such a way as to impart it to them.

A second model is that of a *Bible scholar in a theological school exegeting a text*. This is closely related to the first model but it is so predominant within the more traditional denominations, at least as an ideal for preaching, that it deserves separate mention. Here the effort is to cut beneath popular interpretations and misconceptions and to return to the original meaning of the text. The context in which the passage appears is studied and the world-view of its author is examined. The principal question to be answered is, "How did the writer expect the original readers to understand the words?" The main concern of preaching on this model is to apply appropriate linguistic and historical techniques to the investigation of a Biblical text and thus to increase the hearer's understanding of its original meaning.

The third model in terms of which the function and effectiveness of a sermon can be measured is that of a *speaker providing intellectual stimulation by offering a review of a book or a play or a film*. The work being considered is usually analyzed in such a way as to point to the

19

great human themes which are presented within it. These themes are then, most often, shown to be related to certain life concerns of the listeners.

A fourth image within the popular and professional mind of what preaching is about is the *television news analyst commenting on a current development in world events.* Here the attempt is to help an audience see an incident in its wider context, to clarify its elements, to relate it to historical developments or to show it as a part of larger social movement. In his years as news commentator with CBS, Eric Sevareid was a personification of this model. There may be some expression of personal emotion or opinion in this approach, but the basic attempt is to be fair to all parties and to bring the audience to a broader understanding of the incident.

The fifth model, related to the fourth, is characterized by a far more intense expression of feeling. This is a *social critic calling out against a deplorable social condition and demanding that it be reformed.* A written-word personification of this can be found in some of Philip Wylie's works, principally his *Generation of Vipers.* On this model, preaching is one person daring to stand before a group of other people to make a public exposé of some scandalous corruption, naming names perhaps, giving details and demanding that the situation be made right and that the scoundrels be put to rout. It is more likely that the scoundrels will be distant citizens of the wider community than members present in the congregation. This model is characterized by the feeling tone of moral indignation.

The sixth image, related to the previous two, but more activist, is that of an *action organizer speaking to a group of people and trying to mobilize them to carry out a program of social reform.* The personification of this image is the late Saul Alinsky and the sermon is seen as one Sunday morning technique among many others employed from day to day, all of which the minister uses for the purpose of organizing people into power blocs to bring about some social change. In this model, preaching is essentially talk which seeks to mobilize people into political action.

A seventh image is that of a *salesperson encouraging a client to make a purchase.* Often this type of sermon actually does involve spending money, although usually no object is purchased. This is the fundraising or the membership recruitment sermon. Normally the object of the support is the church itself but the solicitation can be on behalf of an organization of the United Nations or the local United Fund, a group such as Common Cause, a missionary effort or a Service Committee. Finances may not always be the goal; deeper loyalty to the institution may be the intent. But this sermon seeks to "sell a product."

The last of the prevalent models by which a sermon can be composed or evaluated is that of a *physician examining a patient, diagnosing a disease, describing its symptoms and causes, and prescribing a treatment for a cure.* This kind of preaching is found widely all along the denominational and theological spectrum. The fundamentalist preacher is like a physician when speaking about social ills as symptoms of the disease which is human sin and when prescribing a return to scriptures and a renewed faith in Jesus Christ as the cure. The liberal preacher is like a physician when he or she talks about an increase in the divorce rate in the society and suggests that its cause is some malfunctioning in interpersonal communication and that its cure is an increase in openness and honesty or sensitivity to one another. Whether from a fundamentalist or a liberal preacher, the essential elements in this model are that the congregation is sick and the preacher is offering a cure.

These models can provide a new degree of clarity about the preaching transaction. A parishioner complains vaguely that there is something missing from the sermons she hears in her church. Perhaps it will be noticed now that she is listening on the basis of one model of preaching while the preacher is speaking from another model. The parishioner, for instance, wants the preacher to be a physician soothing sick souls, but the preacher wants to be a social critic calling for reform. There is genuine conflict here, but it may find some resolution when the existence and the nature of the implicit models are noticed.

Parishioners and preachers who operate on the model of a professor lecturing to a class are likely to want question and answer sessions to follow the sermons or perhaps will even arrange for occasional sermonless "seminar" Sundays. When, on the other hand, preaching is seen on the Saul Alinsky reform organizer model or on the model of the physician working in a sermon to cure or to

21

soothe distressed souls, cerebral discussions following sermons will be of less interest to both preachers and parishioners.

It should be noticed that each of the models I have presented involves an event, an interpersonal system, a transaction. I do not view the sermon as an object, a manuscript, something which has existence apart from the face-to-face immediate interaction, live, of congregation and preacher. As the script for a play is a thin abstraction for what is experienced in the theatre when the crowd hushes and the house lights dim and the players appear on the stage, so is the manuscript of a sermon a thin abstraction from the fullness and the immediacy of the preaching event. What happens, what transpires in that living event, is composed of what is occurring in the hearts and minds of the hearers as well as what is written on a sheet before the preacher.

A sermon, thus, is a complex, unrepeatable event which takes place in a system formed by a people and a preacher in the context of an occasion of congregational worship. In the preaching event — as in events within a family system or, indeed, any human system — the whole is greater than the sum of its parts, the parts participate in one another, influence is circular, not merely linear, each part of the system influences every other part seasoning the transaction's outcome.

Intent of the Sermon

The models are useful in distinguishing three different possible intentions which may lie behind any given sermon. What outcome is being sought by the preacher? What does he or she wish to have occur within the hearer as a result of having been present when the sermon was delivered?

Of the eight models presented here, the first four have as their intent the increase of knowledge or of sensitivity within the hearers. The college professor lecturing, the Bible scholar examining a text, the reviewer of a book, the news analyst are all models of preaching in which the problem perceived is that the people lack information.

The sermon's intent, then, is to edify by supplying needed information. *Edification* of the congregation is one of the basic intentions of much preaching.

The fifth of the models — the social critic calling out against a social condition and demanding reform — might also have the edification of the listeners as its primary intention. The preacher simply wants the people to know that an unwholesome situation exists, but he or she does not expect the people to do anything about it. If the preacher does expect some action from the people, then the intent of the sermon is no longer simple edification, but is now *motivation*. This is clearly the intent within the sixth and seventh models — the organizer seeking to mobilize people into action and the salesperson encouraging a client to make a purchase.

The third intent characterizes the last of the models — the physician treating the ill patient. Here the preacher is seeking to bring about some personal transformation in the lives of the hearers, a change in their circumstances, release from something that holds them back or binds them in, *liberation*.

While any given sermon, upon analysis, will probably be found to have had a mixture of intentions, I believe that it is possible to classify sermons in terms of their primary intent. Further, I believe that preachers can be separated into three different groups whose preaching-styles and whose general approaches to ministry will cluster about one of these three intentions. There are those whose primary hope, in relation to members of their congregations, is to edify. There are those whose primary hope is to motivate. There are those whose primary hope is to liberate. Preachers might find it a useful experiment in self-discovery to review their past preaching efforts to see which of the three primary intentions have characterized their sermons and if this has changed over the years.

I am not able to say that one of these intentions is proper and the others are not. I know which one characterizes the main thrust of my preaching and my ministry and which one I find most interesting and challenging to work in. It would be useful, I believe, for preachers to increase their awareness of their intention in their sermons. The more aware we are of what we want to do in our preaching, the better preachers we will be.

Liberation

In the remainder of this paper I will explore that approach to preaching whose intent is to encourage a new degree of liberation within the lives of the listeners. I will focus in this way for several reasons: because it is an understanding of preaching which is relatively unexplored; because it reflects the approach to preaching which has been most intriguing and challenging to me in recent years; and because it helps move us beyond those limited conceptions of our nature in which the deepest human difficulties appear to be either ignorance or inertia.

If one believes that ignorance is the primary human problem, one is likely to view the aim of preaching as instruction and edification. If one believes that inertia is the human problem, one is likely to take motivation as preaching's intent. But if one sees as the problem which most significantly diminishes the quality of human experience our tendency to fall into bondages that keep us relatively unfree and relatively unalive, then one will see liberation as the primary aim of preaching.

Preaching, as I understand it and seek to practice it, attempts to lead persons toward an exodus out of their unfreedom and toward a resurrection up from their unaliveness. The preaching which most challenges me is the preaching that seeks to help persons overcome what hypnotherapist Milton H. Erickson refers to as their "learned limitations." It hopes to avoid the empty intellectualizing of some of the preaching which claims to edify. It hopes to avoid, also, the ineffective badgering of some of the preaching which claims to motivate. Its trust is that, when released from bondage to their personal learned limitations, people will begin, on their own, actively to seek edification as their minds are freed to explore. Its trust is, further, that when liberated from their learned limitations, people will be motivated on their own to reach out helpfully toward others as their hearts are freed to love and their wills are freed to act as responsible participants in community.

This trust — that, when freed from the bondage of their learned limitations, people will move, on their own, toward self-actualization and toward responsibility in community — derives for me in part, I am sure, from the positive view of human nature ("the dignity of man") which I learned as a child in the Sunday School of the now disbanded Unitarian Church in Somerville, Massachusetts. This view of human nature as not basically depraved but as full of possibility has found reinforcement beyond Unitarian Universalism in recent years in the work of Abraham Maslow with self-actualizing individuals, in the perspective of Carl Rogers that the basic tendency of the human organism is toward wholeness and health, and in the emphasis on "the possible human" of Fritz Perls, Virginia Satir, Jean Houston, Robert Ornstein and others who have been concerned with human potential and holistic health.

Most recently this outlook on human nature and human transformation has been deepened for me and has been given theoretical grounding[2] by the work of hypnotherapist Milton H. Erickson and by that of a cluster of individuals who have been influenced by the research project in communication theory carried out by Gregory Bateson and others in Palo Alto, California from 1952 to 1962.

One of these, a psychotherapist and a communication theorist, Paul Watzlawick, in an important book, *The Language of Change: Elements of Therapeutic Communication,* draws together concerns of religion, therapy and communication theory. He writes:

> Psychotherapy is concerned with change. But opinions differ widely about what is supposed to change, and these divergences have their roots in the widely different views about the nature of man (*sic*) — and thus in a question that is philosophical, even metaphysical, and not just psychopathological. . . . For the time being, I want to answer the question as pragmatically as possible: Anybody seeking our help suffers, in one way or another, from his relation to the world. Let this mean — borrowing from as far back as early Buddhism which, as we know, was eminently pragmatic — that he suffers from his *image* of the world. . . .[3]

"Let us remember," he writes later, "we never deal with reality *per se* but rather with *images* of reality — that is, with interpretations."[4]

Earlier, in *The Structure of Magic: A Book About Language and Therapy,* in a section entitled "Models and Therapy," Richard Bandler and John Grinder expressed it this way:

25

Our experience has been that, when people come to us in therapy, they typically come with pain, feeling themselves paralyzed, experiencing no choices or freedom of action in their lives. What we have found is not that the world is too limited or that there are no choices, but that people block themselves from seeing those options and possibilities that are open to them since they are not available in their models of their world. . . . Almost every human being in our culture in his life cycle has a number of periods of change and transition which he (sic) must negotiate. . . . What's peculiar is that some people are able to negotiate these periods of change with little difficulty, experiencing these periods as times of intense energy and creativity. Other people, faced with the same challenges, experience these periods as times of dread and pain — periods to be endured, when their primary concern is simple survival. The difference between these two groups appears to us to be primarily that the people who respond creatively to and cope effectively with this stress are people who have a rich representation or model of their situation, one in which they perceive a wide range of options in choosing their actions.[5]

Although preachers do work that differs significantly from that of psychotherapists; although in the sermon they deal with groups of people, not single individuals; although the people do not come to church on Sundays with psychopathological complaints, yet still I believe preachers can learn from what these therapists and communication theorists have discovered. There are some significant areas of overlap. In our preaching we also seek change. We also strive to help people have life and have it more abundantly.

Our calling, our training, our ordination and our standing within the congregation have endowed us with a certain power to influence the way people will interpret reality, to effect change within their images of the world. In our preaching we can provide people with a stimulus to evolve within themselves models and representations of their situation in the world which are liberating of their inner potential, which increase their freedom, which help them become more fully alive, related, creative, actualized.

The Language of the Unconscious

People do not consciously formulate their fundamental images of their world. These grow largely on their own, unconsciously, through a complicated process of experiencing, generalizing, distorting, deleting, and incorporation of the outlooks of others. Watzlawick contends that the "synthesis of our experience of the world into an image is most probably the function of the right hemisphere (of the brain)."[6] Limitation of time does not permit a detailed review of the literature dealing with the phenomena of hemispheric asymmetry and specialization.[7] A summary oversimplification must suffice: the left hemisphere of the brain has to do with logic, counting, computing, language, reasoning; the right hemisphere of the brain, in contrast, specializes in the holistic grasping of complex relationships, patterns and images.

It is Watzlawick's position that people suffer because they are bound in by their images of the world. He holds further that these images are right-hemispheric in origin. He believes, then, that the way for therapists to influence changes in these underlying images, and thus to enable liberation, is through direct interaction with the client's right hemisphere. He criticizes traditional approaches in therapy as overly rationalistic and points to the "inappropriateness of a procedure which essentially consists in translating . . . (the right hemisphere's) analogic language into the (left hemisphere's) digital language of explanation, argument, analyis, confrontation, interpretation, and so forth. . . ."[8] He advises that the way for therapists to induce change is by learning and speaking the enigmatic language of the right hemisphere. The language of the right hemisphere is that of dreams, fairy tales, myth, story, metaphor, analogy, poetry.

Watzlawick's advice to therapists to learn to interact with clients from right hemisphere to right hemisphere recalls Aristotle's observation that, through the imagery of a poem *"cor ad cor loquitur,"* heart speaks to heart. There are momentous implications in this for a new understanding of preaching.

The October 22, 1979 issue of *The New Yorker* reported on a Storytelling Festival which was held in New York City. The editors told of the festival's opening four-hour storytelling session in Central

27

Park and of the passers-by who "stopped and then sat down to listen to one or two stories, and we noticed and remembered that, when people are listening to stories they like, they sit very quietly, their breathing relaxes, and their eyes look big and luminous."[9] The article also carried a Puerto Rican storyteller's reflections on stories she had heard long ago early in her life. "My grandmother had told them to me — stories that kept wonder alive in me. . . . The stories were like kisses from my grandmother, and I loved them, because when I heard them my mind was nothing but pictures."[10]

There is a growing interest in story and other kinds of imagistic communication[11] in many fields of study and I have observed a consensus developing that this form of communication impacts upon hearers in a very different way than does ordinary rational discourse. I believe that the "big luminous eyes" and the relaxed breathing rate that often accompany imagistic communication is the utward sign that right-hemispheric functioning is taking place, the mind "nothing but pictures."

Most preachers surely have observed the deep stillness that develops within their congregation during moments when the communication is particularly imagistic. In such moments many people in the congregation are in an altered mode of consciousness, a trance-like state in which the unconscious (right-hemispheric) mind is actively engaged.

We can observe this, too, in audiences in a theatre. In the first moments after the conclusion of a play, as the house lights come back up, the people blink back from "someplace else." Where have they been?

Poet Robert Frost consistently refused to answer requests to explain in non-poetic language what he meant by a particular poem. "I meant what I said," would be his only reply. Backstage, dancer Isadora Duncan was once similarly asked to tell what she was trying to convey by a dance she had performed. Her reply was like that of the poet: "If I could tell you in words what I meant, I wouldn't have needed to dance it." T.S. Eliot wrote, "The chief use of the (logical connections), the meaning of the poem in the ordinary sense, may be . . . to satisfy one habit of the reader, to keep his mind diverted and quiet, while the poem does its work upon him: much as the imaginary burglar is always provided with a bit of nice meat for the house-dog." Poet Sara Teasdale spoke about this "other" kind or level of communication: "The poet should try to give his poem the quiet swiftness of flame so that the reader will feel and not think while he is reading. But the thinking will come afterwards."

All of these experiences point to the "speaking heart to heart" which takes place through analogy, metaphor, story, imagery — right-hemispheric communication, unconscious speaking directly to unconscious. Powerful liberating preaching engages in this form of communication.

In a valuable book, *Poetry and Experience,* poet Archibald MacLeish recalls William Wordsworth's statement about the way meaning is conveyed through poetry. It is meaning carried "alive into the heart with passion."[12] In two chapters, "Images" and "Metaphor," MacLeish develops his conviction that the "passion" of a poem is not to be understood as mere feeling, but rather as itself a way of knowing. He speaks of "something emotion *knows* — something more immediate than knowledge, something tangible and felt, something as tangible as experience itself. . . ."[13] He asks how a poem creates its truth-bearing emotion in the reader. By the coupling of images, is his answer. The truth of a poem, the emotion of a poem is not contained in an isolated image in the poem, he says. Rather the emotion arises in the space between two or more images juxtaposed.

> No single image can create the . . . emotion . . . , but the juxtaposition of images or image-like statements can create it — and can create it even though — or perhaps because — the juxtaposition is inexplicable to the faculties of reason: men (*sic*) praying with flowers, a laughing girl and a dead doe, the mariners' star and the loyalty of love.[14]

I am suggesting that both art and psychotherapy — and not only preaching — engage in a form of liberating, transformative communication and do it right-hemispherically through the language of the unconscious, through metaphor, story, image. When preachers learn to speak this language, they tap into energies within the congregation that open individuals to new growth and new levels of actualization. When preachers learn this language, they return to what Sallie Te Selle of Vanderbilt Divinity School contends[15] has

29

from time immemorial been the fundamental language of religion: the parable, the metaphor, the myth, the story. The preacher returns again, then, to the roots of religious consciousness, seeking to effect a change in the limited world images in which the listeners are bound. Preaching is a subversive activity — creative but subversive — seeking to stir up and break open the restricting images, to liberate people, to cause to be released in them energies which, because of the narrowness of their image of the world, had been locked in the unconscious.

It is important to note that, while, in this view, the preacher is seen as actively intervening in the lives of the listeners, this intervention is that of a facilitator, not a director. The preacher does not determine life directions for the people but works to expand their underlying images of themselves and their world so that their own inner energies will be released in their lives in self-actualizing and communally responsible ways which are appropriate to them.

It is of concern to me that within Unitarian Universalism there has been a gradual elimination of those very concepts, objects and activities which are most likely to activate right-hemispheric functioning: ritual, symbol, myth, holy book, vestments, ceremonial objects, sacred places and times. The enigmatic and the esoteric have been replaced by the rationalistic and the mundane. This is shaping among us a religion which makes a straight-forward kind of sense to the conscious mind but it is radically decreasing our power to engage the worshipper's unconscious mind. We have liked thinking of ourselves as a religion which speaks to the whole person, but many claim that a human being is some one-tenths conscious and nine-tenths unconscious and I am gravely concerned that our continual insistence on a style of sensible rationalism may be drastically diminishing our ability to speak the language of the unconscious, to speak, that is, to people in their depths.

In a memorandum circulated to his fellow Regents of the University of California, Gregory Bateson made an observation which may have a stunning applicability to contemporary trends within Unitarian Universalist liturgy and preaching. He wrote:

> It is no accident that simultaneously the Roman Catholic Church is giving up the use of Latin, while the rising generation is learning to chant in Sanskrit.[16]

30

Preaching as Sacrament

In the early years of this century, one who stood in relation to the major religion of his land somewhat as we do in relation to that of ours, Congregationalist P. T. Forsyth in Anglican England, wrote:

> To be effective our preaching must be sacramental. . . . If our preaching is not more sacramental than the Catholic altar — I do not say more eloquent or more able, but more sacramental — then it is the altar that must prevail over all our No-Popery. For religion *is* sacramental."[17]

In a 1979 article on preaching,[18] *Time* magazine observed, "For Roman Catholics, the sermon has not been as important (as in Protestantism), but rather a kind of spiritual hors d'oeuvre before the Eucharist." The article reports a Catholic columnist's justification of this. It has been a way, he says, of assuring that priests will not "upstage the Eucharist."

The altar has been removed from most Unitarian Universalist churches and communion, where it occurs at all, is usually a once-a-month observance and even then it is not viewed by many in the congregation as integral to morning worship.

There are those among us who are working to stimulate more richly resourceful, rounded liturgical observances within our congregations. Whatever encouragement we might wish to give such efforts, it is difficult to believe that a reversal is about to take place in the free church tradition's long-held view that preaching is central to worship. Whatever other liturgical developments do take place, it is my hope that the sermon itself will increasingly be seen by preachers as carrying within itself the full force of worship. We can, however, echo Forsyth's sentiment: "But what a task for our preachers to fulfill!"[19] Our traditions have aided us in this; among us, for the most part, the people still look to the sermon expectantly; and perhaps, after all, an altar cannot easily be removed. If the altar goes, the communion table becomes the altar. If the table goes, perhaps pulpit and reading desk begin to take upon themselves the altar's function in worship. And thus unwittingly, the sermon is transmuted into sacrament.

31

I need to indicate more clearly now what I mean by "sacrament." I mean first a very ordinary mundane physical thing. I think of the water used in baptism. I think of the earthly bread and of the fermented juice of the fruit of the vine. A sacrament involves a this-worldly object.

As I understand it from our religious tradition, the sacramental element becomes transformed in the context of the worshiping community. It becomes something experientially more: a medium, a means, a mediator for something else. The traditional formulation holds that a sacrament is a means of grace. In the words of Tillich, the sacraments serve as "media of the Spiritual Presence."[20]

I rush to assure you that I am still referring to what we do when we deliver our sermons. We speak, we do that ordinary human thing; but it is also an awesome thing we do when we do it. I am not referring to an Augustine or a Luther. I am talking about us. I know about the paper and the typewriter or, as in my way, the pencil — the work of preparation. I know about the starting and the stopping, the sweating, the crossing out and the erasing. I know about the interruptions to check a thesaurus or a dictionary, the searching and the waiting for the coming of the right word. And all this makes my point precisely.

The crossed-out, caret-marked essay carried into the pulpit by a sweaty-palmed human being concerned about projecting the voice and emphasizing the proper words: I mean you and me — oh, so very much of *this* world — incomplete in knowledge, not ever as prepared as we might have been for this particular Sunday's venture. I mean us — this-wordly, standing before the waiting congregation with manuscript or outline or scratchings on the back of an envelope — this human person with a tattered essay to share. I mean that precisely *this* is the sacramental element. Not bread, nor wine, nor water, but finite human person standing to give the essay of the morning — this is the sacramental element, mundane, physical, fleshy, finite, faulted. The preacher, herself or himself, is the element in the sacramental act.

A number of times in my ministry, standing near the door greeting members of my congregation after the service, I have watched the approach of an emotion-filled face. And I have then heard words like these: "You touched me. You moved me. You said exactly what I needed to hear — exactly what today I needed to hear. Can I get a copy?" And then I have sent out the copy and some days have gone by and I encounter that person again. "Did you receive the copy of the manuscript I sent?" "Yes, I did," has been the answer, "but it wasn't the right one." How many times has that happened to me in twelve years: four, five, six or more? But I report to you now that it *was* the right one. I assure you that the one I sent was the one requested. And I further assure you that I use a full written manuscript and that I seldom depart at all from what is written there.

Now, how does one explain this? And this experience is the point on which it all begins to turn for me. My guess is that if that sermon had been taped and had been later listened to by that person, it would not seem to be the right one either. What *is* this? What's going on here? A mere trick of memory? An overdose of Sunday emotion? You could say it that way, I suppose, but I want a theological explanation of it and not some psychological or sociological reductionism.

I am enough of an empiricist — a phenomenologist, if you will — to take seriously that person's original report of his and her inner state. I believe that on that Sunday during the sermon that person did indeed hear a word which touched, which moved, a word which said exactly what he or she needed to hear. And I also believe the later report that, upon careful perusal, the word was not to be found anywhere in that manuscript. And my theological explanation of this phenomenon is that, while I was preaching, that person heard a word which no mouth had spoken. From where then? From the brain's right hemisphere? The creative unconscious? Fine! The Holy Spirit? Fine, again!

The believer in the Eucharist, the straightforward unsophisticated believer in the Eucharist. The bell rings. The host is raised and broken. The wine is poured and passed. And suddenly of a special morning, the communicant has a touch of or is filled with a sense of the Real Presence: the body and blood of Christ, the very presence now in his or her own body and spirit of the Most High, maker of heaven and earth. Upon examination later, the wine is seen to be merely wine, the bread to be merely earthly bread. But something has happened. Something of potentially tremendous human significance has happened. "Transubstantiation" it is called.

The turning of earthly elements into the felt presence of the Almighty God.

But the Unitarian Universalist hearer of the sermon doesn't say it that way or think it that way. He or she simply heard a word no mouth had spoken — a healing word, a word of acceptance, of recognition, a word of liberation or of personal reintegration. But that is a momentous event. I am saying that the earthly mundane, sweated-over, tattered essay spoken by this preacher was the element in a sacramental act and that very human moment was — dare I say it? — transubstantiated so that in the experience of that hearer the word of this human preacher became the Word of . . . (no, I don't dare say that). Let me say it this way: while I preached, the person heard a creative, sustaining, redeeming, liberating word. But I did not say that word.

Right hemisphere? Creative Unconscious? Holy Spirit? Almighty God? The Beyond? The Beyond Within? Whatever, wherever, however, preaching which is seen as a sacramental event — preaching viewed on the model of the priest celebrating the Eucharist — is worthy of our continued lively effort and is needed by our people. They look to us expectantly, waiting for something from us, something creative, liberating, enlivening, something that will come to them through us and will make a difference in their lives.

> The people expect the preacher to take them more seriously than they take themselves and they will not thank him (sic) if he does not do so. [21]

34

MIRRORS NEVER LIE?

The Existential Dimensions of Preaching

William F. Schulz

An old Zen teaching tale recalls the time an Emperor once sent for the Wise One to explain the Diamond Sutra. On the appointed day the Wise One appeared at the palace, mounted a platform before the Emperor, rapped once on the table, and then, still not speaking, descended the platform and left. The Emperor sat motionless for a few moments whereupon one of the servants made bold to speak: "Excuse me," inquired the servant, "may I ask whether you understood?" The Emperor sadly shook his head. "What a pity!" the servant exclaimed. "The Wise One has never been more eloquent."

It may well be of course that in many cases silence is more eloquent than sermonizing. Powell Davies used to love to tell the story of the three Scots who were discussing their minister: "We n'er t' 'ad a minister who delved s' deeply int' truth," observed the first. "Aye," said the second. "n' one who stayed down s' long!" "Aye," said the third, "n' one who came up s' dry!" And yet, be that as it may, we still, I think, extend a sympathetic embrace to the Emperor because we Unitarian Universalists are heirs and heiresses to the Western religious tradition and that tradition has from its inception been a verbal one.* I hardly need to construct a homiletical history of Judaism and Christianity to establish the fact that the spoken word, be it in the voice of the prophet expounding law or the voice of the evangelist intoning Christ, has been elemental to the Western religious experience.

Engaging the Word

In the Hebrew scriptures God's second act is an act of speech, second only to the creation of heaven and earth. "And God said, 'Let there be light' and there was light." Until God speaks, the earth, though created, is uninhabitable, "without form and void and darkness is upon [its] face."[2] And God does not simply change all that, does not simply produce the light, but announces good intentions first — speech is somehow necessary to a viable creation. And, furthermore, God's speech is sufficient to fulfill itself: "God said,

---

*As have many Eastern ones as well. "If there were no speech," say the Upanishads, "neither right nor wrong would be known, neither true nor false, neither the pleasant nor the unpleasant. Speech makes us understand all this. Meditate on speech."[1]

'Let there be light' and there *was* light." If any more dramatic evidence of the centrality of speech to the Western religious tradition be required than the first three verses of Genesis, I do not know what it might be. The Christian Scriptures merely confirm the Hebrew — that "In the beginning was the Word . . . and the Word was God."[3]

Little wonder, then, that Jesus, a Jew, did not simply appear before his disciples, rap once upon a table, and depart in silence, but spoke to the people — not as the teachers of old had spoken, to be sure; often in parables, to be sure; often in paradox, to be sure — but *spoke* to them nonetheless. The miracles which he worked, for instance, take place not just with the wave of a hand but with the incantation of a word. "And Jesus, moved with compassion, put forth his hand [to the leper], and touched him, and said unto him, '. . . be thou clean.' "[4] The Sermon on the Mount is a sermon.

And little wonder that the Apostle Paul, promoting his new-found Gospel throughout the ancient world, should regard preaching as the most effective means of its propogation — more effective than prayer; more effective than ritual. "Preach the word," Paul advises Timothy, "in season, out of season; reprove, rebuke, exhort, with all long-suffering . . ."[5]

Now that is quite a charge but one which Paul and Timothy and most of their latter-day counterparts have taken up with confidence: "Reprove, rebuke, exhort, with all long-suffering . . ." No doubts or quandaries; the Gospel message is quite clear. Obviously here are preachers who preach with assurance; preachers who *know* what to preach. No pop psychology for preachers such as these; no temporal topicality; no book review sermon this week. (Or perhaps more accurately, a book review sermon every week but always the same book.) Surely it was a minister of this ilk who, having preached a magnificent sermon, well received one week, is reputed to have entered the pulpit the following Sunday, pounded the desk, and said to the congregation: "My friends, I repeat what I said last week."[6] The Word, the Gospel, the Truth precedes its own articulation. The falsity of its speaker's voice cannot corrupt it any more than the personal shortcomings of the priest corrupt the Host. The *Logia* is safe, despite the theological confabulations of the centuries. Its origin is ancient; its power, plain; its meaning, grand.

38

For we Unitarian Universalists, however, the matter is not so simple for, regardless of our theological persuasions, we know that *we* are the authors of our words; that, even when we preach the Gospel, it is a Gospel fashioned out of our fragility; that, even when we rely on the Holy Spirit, it is we and not the Spirit who must answer for our failings.

This means that who we, the preachers, *are*, is almost — not quite — but almost as important as what we preach. For we are not just the agent of the Ultimate (though we may well be that) and not just the purveyor of some ancient creed, but the very crucible in which the religious drama — of doubt and despair; forgiveness and faith — is being played. No wonder then that we so-called "liberal" preachers are subject to anxiety; no wonder that we are sometimes inadequately burdened by humility. Because for preachers such as us, unlike for Paul or Timothy, the Word itself depends upon our very being.

Paul told the Corinthians "Preach not yourselves but Christ Jesus."[7] But for us, even to "preach Christ" means to preach Christ by and through ourselves, through our *experience*; we know no other way. The Word does *not* precede its enunciation or, if it does, we cannot know it. We can of course know others who have pronounced it long before us but even that testimony does not come alive until we live it.

Our job, as preachers, then, is not just to scour the tradition and be its vocal amanuensis. Our job is to engage the tradition in a struggle with the world. Our job is to engage the Gospel with our lives and then, invoking faith, proclaim a word. And if our voice be false, that word is thereby tainted. The task is not unlike God's task in Genesis: to take the creation of the world, so blessed, and make it viable (literally, "liveable") by our speech. No wonder, then, that we are subject to anxiety; no wonder that we are sometimes inadequately burdened by humility. But no wonder also that to preach under the auspices of our sanction is to be offered an opportunity unlike any other.

The Anxieties of Preaching

The passion to be listened to lurks just beneath the skin of every preacher. Perhaps this is why some pulpiteers have such difficulty bringing their sermons to conclusion, for conclusion signals the disappearance (for this week at least and, who knows, perhaps forever) of their (presumably) appreciative audience. From this point of view it is certainly unfortunate that brevity and a snappy ending are such valued characteristics of the preacher's trade. It has been said that all the sermons ever delivered over the years at Oxford University have been divisible into four categories, distinguished respectively for Altitude, Latitude, Platitude, and Longitude. It has been said further that all were tolerated except the last.[8] And I'm afraid it really is true that the best test of a preacher is not too different from what Wellington considered the best test of a general: "To know when to retreat and how to do it!" Paul Carnes used to say that a rip-roaring conclusion could salvage even the most dismal sermon.

Make no mistake, however: it is not bad to want to be listened to. Indeed, if the preacher herself does not care for her message, why should anyone else? "The crucial question," a Harvard Divinity School professor used to tell his students, "is, 'How far would you go to hear yourself preach?'" Isn't one reason that more and more women are finding the ministry a compatible profession because it offers them a voice and a forum when before their voices were more private than public, their forums more constrictive than free? In any case, for man or woman the yearning to be heard is primal to the preacher's psyche.

As with all such passions, this one is accompanied by its corresponding hazards. The first of course is the fear of *not* being listened to. The second is the fear of being listened to too much.

Surely one of the deepest anxieties which afflicts every person, whether preacher or not, is the concern that what we have to say and how we say it will not be found worthy. The perennial minister's nightmare of entering the pulpit only to discover that one has lost one's notes is reflective not just of a fear of being unprepared but of the deep-rooted conviction that, without those notes, without that preparation, we really have nothing to say. I know one or two preachers who *claim* not to care how many people attend a service in which they occupy the pulpit but I know none whose testimony on this point I am willing to believe. And why should we not care? For if we have labored mightily and rent our souls for the sake of a sermonic work, why ought we not care that as many as possible experience that creation?

The hazard comes of course with what I have described as our notion of the word for, if our sermons are at least in part reflective of our religious struggles, then a congregation's rejection of our preaching is not simply a rejection of the doctrine we pronounce but a rejection of our very selves. It is not just then that "what we have to say and how we say it" will not be found worthy. It is that *who I am* may not be either. It is a fool, therefore, who, before entering the pulpit, fails to pause and tremble.

And yet this anxiety — that we and what we offer may not be well received — is a fairly useful anxiety at that. For one thing it may serve as corrective to the conceit just mentioned that everything we have to say deserves to be said at length. The longer we speak, the more we put our selves at jeopardy. For another thing it may keep our sermons interesting.

And yet sometimes we communicate too well. The second anxiety which accompanies the passion to be listened to is the fear of being listened to too closely. If there is one thing worse than having one's message ignored, it is having it taken to heart, truly to heart.

The last thing which ministers of our tradition want is for parishioners to place their lives wholly in our hands. Our authority, though real, is limited and this cuts both ways. Sometimes, I know, we wish that we could be perceived as seraphim and wonder only that our congregations are so blind as to miss our wings. But most of the time we are just as relieved to realize that the image of shepherd and sheep is foreign to our faith and that our goal is to increase the people's empowerment, not dependence. The reason we are relieved is because we know that the moment we stop preaching what in retrospect will seem at least a little foolish, at just that moment we have ceased as individuals to grow and change. And the preacher's growth — in personal maturity, in religious depth, in

41

worldliness and lack of worldliness, in the capacity to strike a telling metaphor or to strike an awkward phrase — is barometric to his or her success.

A sermon differs from a lecture. Our task is not just to impart some information. Our task is to call the people to an experience of the Profound through the drama of the tradition as manifested through our lives and faith. It is not enough to know everything about a topic, to read every book, relish every expert, and declare the findings with wit and zest if we cannot at the same time tell the congregation why it matters, why we care, how we've lived the matter and how it's enlivened us. It is not enough to proclaim the goals and purposes of life, ideals to emulate, the ends of faith, if we do not at some point also share our failures and false starts, the process by which we, as pilgrims, have trod the appointed ground.

Soren Kierkegaard relates a story about the world's greatest theologian who had written a famous book proving to everyone's satisfaction that God is Love. The book found its way into the studies of virtually all the ministers on the continent and informed their preaching and their pastorates. But then one day the theologian underwent a personal crisis, a crisis which made him doubt that God indeed was Love, and so he sought out a member of the clergy, hitherto unknown to him, to whom he himself was hitherto unknown, and put the crisis squarely: "Here is what has happened in my life," he said. "Now tell me: how do *you* know that God is love?" Still not knowing the identity of his guest, the minister smiled smartly, stepped over to the bookshelf, and, pointing to the theologian's *magnum opus,* said, "Here is a book which proves that God is Love. Read it, study it, and if it does not help you, nothing can."[9] What a pity that that minister did not share the conviction of the Bishop of Massilon who, when asked which were his greatest sermons, replied, "The ones I know best in my heart."

Yet this conviction too — that we need mirror our experiences in order to help the people recognize theirs — is fraught with anxious consequences. Do mirrors ever lie or, conversely, do they sometimes tell too much?

Every preacher knows the agony of matching words to music when the congregation knows the score. Every minister lives under the judgment of his or her own principles. Every word of self-disclosure risks the later charge of fraud.

The salve to this anxiety is that the more regularly we preach — particularly to one congregation — the more we are forced to work out our theology, our principles, to resolve its kinks and contradictions and then the more we preach it, the more we may believe and live it for ourselves. "Preach faith until you have it," urged John Wesley, "And then, because you have it, you will preach faith." In this sense preaching can be self-fulfilling, like God's command, "Let there be light!" For a good preacher is never preaching solely to the people; every good preacher preaches also to herself.

It is harder to be a hypocrite — still possible, to be sure, but harder — if one's words are down in black and white. To speak the faith as best I know it in my heart and to confess the ways in which the gracious eludes me too is to vivify the religious drama for myself and, if it does not come alive for me, I can hardly expect to make it live for someone else. On more than one occasion tears have filled my eyes when I was speaking. It was not because the words were beautiful (for pretty words are often affectation). It was rather, I think, because the words were true — not necessarily true as the world would call them but true to the peculiar fidelities which are myself. Mirrors sometimes lie of course but congregations are generally well attuned to an authentic voice and, given time, can readily tell a true from false reflection.

There is another problem though with this mirror image and that is when the mirror tells too much, when the preacher is so self-absorbed that there is no room in the mirror for anyone else. The reason, after all, to share my own adventure is to elucidate the peoples', not to immortalize myself. There has to be a difference between a sermon and a soap opera. Worse even than cold and distant sermons are sermons smarmy with tales of self, wallowing in the glory of the preacher's pain. The best mirrors never lie, it's true, but neither do they tell too much.

The Marks of "Great" Preaching

To this point I have been dealing with the relationship of the preacher to the preaching act. I believe that in our preaching who we are is almost — but not quite — as important as what we preach. Authenticity is a necessary but not sufficient quality of "great" preaching. To deserve that appellation, our sermons must be characterized by three additional conditions. They must be *true;* they must be *evocative;* they must be *transforming.*

"Truth is the power that is to conquer the world," proclaimed William Ellery Channing, and he went on to advise young preachers that the truth of what they say is infinitely more important than how they say it. "I would caution you," he warned, ". . . against efforts to startle or dazzle . . . There is no more effective security against dullness than [simple] truth."[10]

In the intervening years since Channing's day, however, the type of truth of which he spoke — bold, objective, certain — has fallen into disrepute. Faith statements have replaced truth claims as the *sine qua non* of religious language. Within our movement in particular, the worship of pluralism and our refusal (or inability) to set boundaries to what is acceptable Unitarian Universalist belief has appeared to make the question of a sermon's truth or falsity virtually meaningless. How can we label another person's words as "false" if we cannot provide a satisfactory answer to Pilate's famous question, "What is truth?" How can we judge the accuracy of a preacher's presentation if no greater claim for it is made than that of personal testimony?

This is not the place to offer an epistemology for religious liberalism — much as it is needed and even if I knew the way. But I do want to affirm the legitimacy of evaluating a sermon in part on the basis of whether it is true. Not true in the strict apodictic sense that Channing had in mind: that its observations correspond to "reality." (To the extent that a preacher cites facts of course, those facts had better be as accurate as possible — and, indeed, some of the most stirring sermons consist of little more than an artful recitation of powerful and telling facts — but most serons are too much like poems to depend strictly on facts for their vitality.) But "true" in another sense.

For me the image which begins to get at the type of truth which good preaching embodies is the image of weaving. I am indebted to feminism for this image and, more specifically, to Adrienne Rich who speaks in one of her poems of discovering an old piece of a grandmother's patchwork, never finished, and of taking up the work where the grandmother had left off:

> This weaving, ragged because incomplete
> we turn our hands to, interrupted
> over and over, handed down
> unfinished, found in the drawer
> of an old dresser in the barn,
> her vanished pride and care
> still urging us on
> our work . . .
> to help the earth deliver.[11]

There are two ways in which the image of weaving seems right to me. First, because a true sermon is a tapestry drawn from tradition, memory, conversations long forgotten, candor, courtesy, pain and passion, fresh insight and fresh metaphor, but all united around some common theme, some base conviction, some urgent message, some thread of faith, which centers and energizes all that I would say. It is too simple to suggest, as the old chestnut has it, that every minister has but one sermon with a hundred variations, but every minister does need to have at least the semblance of a coherent theology, consonant with the tradition of our church and communicable in a tongue we understand.

Such a theology must be faithful to the grandmothers while at the same time it moves us further toward the delivery of the earth. In this sense every sermon which is true *will* be but an elaboration upon that basic design, for otherwise it falls apart at the seams and we are left with the silliness of an Emerson who, while preaching an old sermon written many years before, is reputed to have stopped suddenly in the middle of it, said to the congregation, "The sentence which I have just read I do not now believe," and gone on reading the sermon. Sermonic truth is in part a function of the clarity and consistency of the central grain.

And the image of weaving seems appropriate in another way: because a sermon which is true weaves an elaborate web between preacher, congregation, and profundity such that all three are caught up in a kind of whole-some pattern, connected by common elements of language, values, concepts, and concerns. Part of a

45

preacher's job is to provide the people tools — the flax and the loom, if you will — with which to gain access to the deeper dimensions of their humanity and with which to carry on a religious conversation with each other. This is the way sermons contribute to the creation of a community and the truth of a sermon can be judged in part by whether it effects such resonance.

A Marxist student at Smith College once told Professor Jean Elshstain that "to raise a child is merely to reproduce a future commodity for the labor force" and Elshstain replied, "Is that why I'm scared when my child goes bike riding? Because capitalism may be losing a wage earner? Tell me another." To this degree the people determine the truth or adequacy of the web the preacher tries to weave. Thornton Wilder once observed that "If Queen Elizabeth or Frederick the Great or Ernest Hemingway had read their own biographies, they would exclaim, 'Ah, my secret is still safe!' But if Natasha Rostov, a character in Tolstoy's *War and Peace*, were to read that book, she would cry out as she covered her face with her hands, 'How did he know? How did he know?' " And that is also the exclamation which the people make when the pattern fits, when the sermon's true: "How did you know? How did you know?"

A great sermon, however, need not only be true, for truth can be pedestrian and the people have been known to be deceived. In addition to being true, our words must also be evocative of something beyond the present-ness of the day. Frost said that "a great poem reminds us of what we almost didn't know we knew." One of my colleagues has similarly pointed out that a great sermon says for the congregation what they almost didn't know they had to say. [12]

A religious person is, by definition, a "being toward the future," [13] like a grandmother's patchwork: beloved but incomplete. Religion by its very definition has to do with values yet realized, possibilities not yet named, splendors not yet seen. The good life, when and if it finally comes, is always different from our expectations. "My own suspicion," said J.B.S. Haldane, "is that the universe is not only queerer than we do suppose but also queerer than we can suppose." In light of all this, the preacher can do little more than hint at those glories and imperatives which command our fealty.

But hinting is enough. It is enough to kindle in the people a sense of freedom long discarded, of loves and sorrows too soon displaced.

46

It is enough to disclose a miracle amid the banal, to save the epiphanous from the mundane.

The author Gloria Fox grew up in the household of a minister. One Sunday when she was six years old, the minister asked her what he should preach about that week. "A waterfall!" said Gloria because her picnic had recently been dampened by the spray from a cascade. "I can still recollect the startled pleasure," she later wrote, "when, sitting in the corner of a pew that Sunday, I realized that his sermon was indeed about a waterfall. Of course I knew nothing about metaphors or themes. But for an instant I grasped [the fact] that everything could count, that a word, spoken as meant, contained in itself the energy to awaken almost anything — imagination, thought, emotion — just as in the Chinese soapstone I often held in my hand, there was the concentrated essence of an earthquake." In a sermon which is true, the people sit up, take notice, resonate. In an evocative sermon the people quake.

But not with fear. With the recognition of their capacity to change. This is the final hallmark of a great sermon: that it contributes to a transformation. No sermon alone can redeem a battered life or repair a shattered world but it can surely signal the direction. An ontological assumption accompanies every preacher into every pulpit: the assumption that we human beings possess the capacity to choose a better life. Without that assumption, there is simply no point, no point at all, of preaching "good news to the poor . . . , release to the captives," no point in "proclaiming the acceptable year of the Lord."[14] The preacher's job is to awaken the people's vision of that better way to be and to make more available to them the means to get there. The people's responsibility in return is to make a decision whether to deny that vision and that power or to make them manifest in a renewal of faith or witness or integrity.

A transforming sermon always offers the assurance that the margins are wider than we think; that the world, even in its agony, retain an option; that a person, even facing death, can seal a triumph. There is a painting somewhere in a European gallery of the scene in which Faust sits opposite the Devil at a chess table. Faust's face is contorted in anguish for he retains on the board but a knight and the King and the King is in check. Thousands of people have walked by this painting, aware that in the very next move the Devil will secure the victory. But one day a chess master happened by to stop and stare. The minutes changed to hours but still the master stared. Then suddenly, "It's a lie!" he screamed, "The King and the knight have another move! They have another move!" That is the message, too, of a sermon which transforms.

The Worthiness of Preaching

These, I hold, are the characteristics of great preaching: that our words be authentic, true, evocative, and transforming. Let me add quickly that very few, if any, of my own sermons have been all four. I feel fortunate if I can satisfy but two. Thomas Wolfe advised aspiring novelists to "Always write masterpieces . . . There's a better market for them!" Fortunately sermons are not like novels: they are far from the sole factor upon which the value of a ministry is based. And congregations are not like critics: they are often able to find the most surprising wheat in the midst of the most tattered chaff. "Many are the ministers," a Methodist bishop once observed, "who are only a cinder of what they might have been if they had not been blown upon all their lives by the bellows of undiscriminating praise."[15]

Yet, be that as it may, the preaching event, the proclamation of a word, *does* make creation habitable. "Speech," wrote Thomas Mann in *The Magic Mountain*, "is civilization itself. The word — even the most contradictory word — preserves contact. It is silence which isolates." Surely this is as worthy a project as any that can be imagined: to crack our human isolation with a sentence which sustains. For all that preserves the world is thereby given promise: that though woe will often triumph, a dream remains.

THE WIZARDRY OF WORDS:
Preaching and Personal
Transformation

Joyce H. Smith

Do we want to change people with our preaching? Do we want to be wizards in the pulpit?

Six years ago I preached a sermon on hunger. I suggested that, inasmuch as the growing of beef cattle takes the greatest number of resources (in terms of available soil, nutrients and labor) of all food products, the consuming of beef may show a lack of concern about the food needs of the people in our world. I noted that this was particularly relevant to those of us in the United States since we have the highest per capita consumption of beef of any nation. The sermon was fact-filled and emotion-laden. Several months later I had a surprising repercussion from that sermon. One of the church members who had heard it called me after our annual fellowship dinner. He was angry because we had served beef at the dinner. He told me that, since hearing my sermon on hunger, he had cut beef out of his diet in an attempt to be responsible by eating lower on the food chain. And here was *his* church serving beef!

I was taken aback — not by the criticism (which was apt), but by the hitherto unknown effectiveness of my words. I had changed someone! Had you asked me if that is what I had wanted my sermon to do, I might well have answered, "No." Of course I had not changed my congregant's basic values. He had long believed that he should have a caring and responsible relationship with this world. What I had changed was his behavior by opening up a new understanding of how his behavior might affect others.

If you do not want to change people, don't preach. If you do preach, then be as responsible as possible for the changes you may make. All communication changes us. We are continually processing our experiences, information and emotions, putting them into meaning systems that shape our lives. We need to know how change comes about.

Understanding Change

Often when we preach to people, we are simply reinforcing their present values and behavior, as in my story. According to Robert Tapp in his 1966 survey, 77% of the Unitarian Universalists interviewed reported that they came to church with their values already formed.[1] This study suggests that our people are not looking to religion to provide change. They are looking for clarification, enlargement and support of their current values. What our members are seeking is to maintain values and world views in the midst of competing values and world views. What they are seeking is to understand the dimensions of their faith, to weather those personal and social changes which are a part of each person's life . . . and to do so with an increasing sense of centeredness.

Sometimes our preaching may simply encourage a person to go in the direction which she or he has already chosen. Preaching of this order is often only a matter of removing road blocks or disclosing new paths. Occasionally, however, our words may have the effect of a lightning flash or the power of a strange potion. Whether the changes we provoke are gradual or climatic, we need to know the wizard's trade with its potency as well as we can.

Many of our theories of change and how it takes place come from the disciplines of education and therapy. These disciplines offer ideas as to how to change others or how to allow them to "grow themselves." Many of these theories are restatements of old truths practiced by religions for centuries. The weekly therapy session, private or group, attests to the need for regular meetings of a support group. Self-revelation is part of confession and therapy. Resistance to change is recognized in religion, education and therapy. An examination of the past to find out its effects on the present and future has long been part of religious practice. Education has discovered mentors and role models whereas saints and gurus were formerly models for emulation. The beginnings of understanding how sensory participation is important for change will be discussed later. Religion has used sensory participation — sight, smell, taste and touch — in a variety of ways to evoke the power to change. Therapy and education help religion by a self-conscious incorporation of methods which religions discovered intuitively.

There are three underlying assumptions to this paper:

1) Change in itself is neither good or bad; it is a normal part of living. There are particular changes, however, which can be good or bad, helpful or harmful, to the maintenance of an individual's life, a social group's existence, or the continuation of the human species.

2) Change takes place in three arenas: physical, social and symbolic. Changes in all three areas may be sudden or gradual. In the physical world we experience biological changes and changes in our surroundings: we experience sudden changes like birth, puberty, death, volcanoes, earthquakes, floods and gradual changes like growth, aging, erosion, adaptation to new circumstances.

Social changes too may be abrupt (as in marriage, separation, war, revolution) or gradual (as in fads, lawful government changes, or the changing status of professions, age groups, sexes).

Symbolic changes can come suddenly, as in an experience of religious conversion or a major scientific discovery (such as Newton's or Einstein's physics or the recognition that the earth travels around the sun) although the absorption of these new world views may be gradual (as is the recognition of the earth's vulnerability, as captured by the television symbol of the earth as a fragile, toy-like "Blue Marble"). Religious symbols may gradually change as from an earth goddess to the Virgin Mary.

All three of these arenas of change are deeply interrelated and we cannot undetstand how change takes place unless we respect their interrelations. The sermon takes place in all these worlds at once. It is a physical event in a social context which shapes word symbols which in turn reshape how we experience our social and physical world.

3) Experiences are many-layered. Not only are there physical, social and symbolic layers to our experience, but there are probably developmental layers as well. I do not hold strictly to James Fowler's faith development theories[2] (which are in turn based on theories of Piaget and Kohlberg) but I do accept the idea that each one of us throughout our lives continually experiences new ways of understanding and "putting together" our life experience. Former syntheses undoubtedly continue to exist within us. This concept is very important when we deal with what happens in the sermon experience. Former world views, former ways of perceiving our world, reside within us and can be triggered and reactivated by stimuli, including powerful word images. These former worlds are the powerful unknown memory factors with which we deal.

One of the most common times when we touch a past synthesis of childhood is in grief experience. When an important person has died, the grieving person is thrust into the feelings and dependency of the child-state. Reactions are often in the form of a child's world view: "I must have caused the death by some bad thought or act" or "I am being punished for something I did" or "I don't deserve to live." Even a person whose belief system does not consciously contain these views may find the child's synthesis come rushing to the surface in times of grief. Many religions have fed on these dependency views by taking the role of the "good loving parent" or the "punitive parent making judgments." We Unitarian Universalists do not intentionally reinforce these views in our religious teaching but we must be aware of their power and potential eruption, not only in the grief process but at times of vulnerability in a person's life.

Building on these three assumptions about change, I would suggest that there are two prerequisites for change to take place in the religious setting, as well as in therapy or education. First, we must establish a climate of trust, and, second, we must establish a climate of valuing.

A Climate of Trust

Preachers, teachers or therapists must inspire trust in the people whom they approach in order for those people to be willing to risk change. Trust does not mean that you, the preacher, are always right or always loving. Trust means that you are one who will not deliberately be false to either facts or attitudes or to your own beliefs or self. Trust means you will not deliberately use your power to mislead or harm or destroy. This climate of trust is so axiomatic that we often forget its importance in preaching. Such trust underlies the ongoing religious community. If the climate of trust is broken, no matter how good the sermons may be, they are probably no longer powerful in the lives of that community. The climate of trust is harder for the one-time preacher to create. Yet for every new person walking through the door of the church, you are the one-time preacher who needs to create trust. The hearer, new or old, comes with at least a tentative trust just by being there.

As one who constantly speaks in different churches, I know the added tension of being in a community in which the climate of trust cannot be taken for granted. I am aware that I must create the climate myself. My credentials as a denominational official may actually create a climate of distrust rather than work in my favor.

Trust must be established at the beginning of a sermon. The attitude and manner of the preacher are important. If the setting is too strange or unfamiliar, distrust may be created. If symbols and rituals generate negative reactions among the congregants, bringing unhappy memories to mind, distrust may enter.

Because I often preach to an unfamiliar congregation, I usually insist on doing at least one of the readings before the sermon in order to gain the congregation's trust. One minister tells a humorous story (not necessarily connected to the subject) at the beginning of each sermon — a practice which may be designed to relieve the minister's mistrust as much as the congregation's! Another minister works slowly into his subject because he feels that abruptness will put people on guard. As a method of trust building, I come out from behind the pulpit, making myself vulnerable rather than protected. That act has been misread, however. One congregant told me that he was very anxious when I walked out from behind the pulpit. The unfamiliar action in that case was evidently threatening rather than trust-building. Or perhaps stepping out of the pulpit decreased my claim to authority.

The tone of voice is one of the most effective ways to create trust. Confidence, warmth, directness and openness of tone give the message, "I am trustworthy. It is safe to listen to me." Any actor can learn such a tone; it is one of President Reagan's greatest assets. The preacher living in a community, however, will need to match his or her life to the words for, no matter how good an actor s/he is, a pose will not last long under the scrutiny of an involved community. The denomination's recognition through the Ministerial Fellowship Committee and a minister's schooling and calling are all part of the trust-building process.

A Climate of Worth

Second only to trust is our communication of a genuine belief that our hearers are worthy. To change requires of human beings the feeling that they have some capability to change and are to some degree loved. In order to risk incorporating new learnings, to listen

55

with a receptive self, to be in new ways, the hearer must have an assurance of his/her own worth.

The older Universalists created a feeling of worth by preaching God's powerful love, no matter what a person's condition; the Unitarians breathed into people the sense that they could know and do the good. Those traditions are still sources for us to draw upon today. Whatever the source of this sense of being of worth for you — whether it is a belief that each is a child of God, touched with divinity, or a part of an ever more complex evolving universe — whatever the theological source for you, you must evoke that sense of worth to empower people to change. Unitarian Universalists may appear to be self-confident, assured of their worth and lovableness, but many will come to church with a deep sense, whether it be permanent or transient, of being of little worth, unloved and un-lovable, incompetent or not OK.

Having helped to create these two climates — trust and a feeling of worth — in which change can occur, how does change happen? In two ways: first, new experiences change us, and, secondly, new explanations and pictures of the meaning of our experience change us.

The new experience which may be presented in the religious community is precisely that sense of a climate of trust and accept-ance which I have been describing. If the preacher can create this in her/his sermons and service and if the congregation can build that same feeling in the community life of the group, this new experience may be brimming with change potential. The religious group may be one of the few settings where this trust and acceptance is expe-rienced. The sermon is partly a modeling of what the community should act out. In our churches we are very familiar with the new sense of freedom some people feel: "Here I can doubt and express my doubts. Here the preacher raises questions I never thought of. Here I am accepted as I really am." This is a commonly reported experience at new members' meetings. Our testimonials often rival those of a born-again conversion experience and such an experience is freeing.

The major function of the sermon is to change the understanding of, or symbolized meaning of, our experience; the pictures in our head which tell us how we can interpret our reality and how we

56

should act as a result. The remainder of this paper will deal with this kind of wizardry.

In the process of affecting the symbolized meanings of our experience, the use of the story in the sermon is a vital ingredient. The story ties the abstract symbols and concepts to the concrete experience in everyday life. Roy Phillips in his paper "Preaching as a Sacramental Event"[3] tells us that in the process of storytelling, the right brain is touched by images and pictures and this allows us to be aware of the right-brain understanding which adds to our cognitive, reasoning understanding.

Changing Through Stories

In his book *Building the Word*,[4] J. Randall Nichols describes another way of looking at what happens in storytelling. As the message of the preacher is unfolded in a story which provides the context for her/his good news, the inner story of the listener is touched. Experiences from the past flood into the awareness of the hearer. As the story unfolds, the hearer relives the story which is personally hers or his. As Nichols says, "The incoming message is partly *appropriated* into our unfolding stories, with or without distortion, and our stories themselves partly *accommodate* themselves to the incoming message. When the experience is over, neither the message nor our inner story is quite what it started out to be, and in that interplay is the dynamic of the communication process."[5]

Roy Phillips tells of an experience which has happened several times to him. A congregant is deeply moved by a sermon and asks for a copy. The sermon is sent and later, when Roy asks if the person received the sermon, the parishioner says vaguely, "Oh, yes, but it wasn't the right one; it was not the one I heard."[6] Indeed, the sermon which parishioners hear is seldom the one which a minister has preached because the preacher's stories are always modified by the stories of the hearers. Something new has happened — not only the blending of the stories of preacher and congregant into a new synthesis but also, in the memory of the hearer, an actual change can take place in the story.

Consider the example of a parishioner who hears a story which triggers the childhood memory of feeling rejected by his father. He

57

remembers being scolded severely for interrupting his father's important work. The feelings of rejection from that childhood experience continue to influence the behavior of the grown man whenever he is criticized. The sermon tells a different story, however: that of a father who had no time for his children as they grew up and who now wants their love and friendship and regrets the distance and alienation of his grown children. The new sermon story can blend into the story from the hearer's past and actually change the remembered experience of the past, freeing the hearer of the intense feelings of rejection. Such a restructuring of the effect of past memories may be what true forgiveness means.

I think that such a restructuring is possible because I have participated in two workshops given by Richard Bandler in which he has used some physical techniques to change past memories. The process, simply stated, involves first remembering an intense, pleasant emotional experience which the therapist "anchors" on some part of the body with a firm touch! That touch on that same spot can bring back the good memory and its emotion even in the face of unpleasant remembrances. This is demonstrated when an unpleasant memory is brought to mind. As this unpleasant experience is remembered, pressure on the spot of the "anchored" pleasant memory overlays the unpleasant memory and actually changes it in the mind of the participant. I have experienced this process myself. Bandler teaches therapists a process which helps people change the hold of past memories over present behavior.

Bandler worked out his ideas by watching the work of skilled therapists like Virginia Satir. He tells of observing Satir as she worked with an unhappy married couple. Satir encouraged the couple to discuss those problems which usually led them to begin a quarrel. In the middle of the quarrel, she positioned herself between the husband and wife so that neither of them could any longer see the anger of the other. Then she touched the man on the knee, saying, "Remember for me the first time you fell in love with your wife." When the man had gone into that memory and it was firmly associated with the pressure on the knee, Satir moved out from between the two people and asked them to resume their "discussion." As they did so, Satir kept her hand on the man's knee, where the thoughts of love had been anchored. The wife, still angry, was suddenly faced with a husband whose face showed love and the quarrel melted away. The communication between the two people had changed.

This sounds gimmicky until you remember occasions when someone has grabbed you by the arm in a particular way and, for apparently no reason at all, you felt intensely angry, or when someone has hugged you or patted you on the back as most babies are patted when they are comforted by parents, and you felt comforted. Such anchors to the past memories do exist, in touch and sight and word. And Jesus knew the power of the unexpected reaction when he recommended that his followers respond to a slap on the cheek by turning the other. He knew instinctively that such an act could change the relationship.

Preachers, just as skilled therapists, can and do anchor new ways of remembering, often without what they do. A tone of voice, slower speech, the right word for the community can evoke certain emotions. For me the expressions "Jeeesus!" or "Gaawd!" are spoken negative triggers which get in the way of deep awe or love but for some people they are positive triggers to deep religious feelings. We, too, may have words which evoke a mystical or loving reaction. The names "Emerson," "Thoreau," and "Starr King" may anchor certain positive responses for us.

We begin to get a sense of why the use of strong sensual images in storytelling is important. The words themselves are triggers to the senses which store memories. Marcel Proust had such a strong sensual memory that the odor of perfume, a movement of blue water, a strain of Beethoven, a rustle of silk on the stair would evoke in him a complete picture of a past scene.

The actors, emotions and situation flowed back to Proust as though they were happening at that very moment.

We can evoke a past, schemes of beliefs and ways of living, by the "sound pictures" we paint. A skilled visual artist such as Stanley Kubrick can use costumes, furniture, buildings, sky and weather to evoke a time and place and make us live in that vision. We experienced the plastic barrenness of modernity in A Clockwork Orange; the strangeness of a future time in 2001; and the sense of slow, laborious time in the languor of Barry Linden. Our society has become so oriented to the visual that we word wizards often wonder if we must use the visual to be more effective in conveying our meanings.

The visual may be useful but, as word wizards, we can evoke this rich visual experience which our hearers possess to convey meaning verbally. Our congregations have seen more things than any previous age. The camera's eye has shown us other cultures, wide worlds, animals and insects, cells of our bodies and galaxies of the universe. It is up to us preachers to take those images and weave meanings with threads of that shared experience, evoking delight, wonder, power, love and caring. The poet can teach us that the word is both an evoker of other sensual experience and an experience in itself. Nonsense rhymes and rhythms of religious chants tell us that the sound itself is a rich resource of meaning. The poet uses unexpected juxtapositions of words to create new insights. We can juxtapose new similes in the same way. One minister I know has used the *Wizard of Oz* as a simile for ministry and I have used Charlie Brown as an example of one who speaks the truth in love compared to Lucy, who only speaks the truth. The surprise of finding the new meaning in an old place splits open the wine skins and makes us drink that wine whose intoxication changes us and our world.

Another function of stories and the use of sharp sensual images is to make us aware of the many-layered nature of this world which we so often think is a simple one. For centuries we have divided ourselves into bits and pieces, such as mind, body, soul, ego, id, superego. Harvard's Professor James Fowler tells us that we move through stages of faith development similar to Piaget's stages of cognitive development and Kohlberg's ideas about moral development. The scientific mind's desire for dissection and the logician's desire for discrete packaging make these stages and pieces seem discontinuous. I see the self, rather, as a dish of chocolate revel ice cream. There are layers of development but they flow into one another and often shoot to the surface or sink to the bottom in wavy undulations. We touch and evoke these layers in religious rituals and services. The four-year-old child cannot distinguish the *talk* about robbers from the fear that they will walk into the door at any moment. This is the same development stage which equates the thinking of bad thoughts about a person and the actual killing of that person. And yet such magical thinking underlies the notion of transubstantiation in which wine becomes holy blood and bread, the divine body infusing the believer with the good.

The development stage which desires a we-they sense of belonging is reaffirmed in the community of faith. The need to see right and wrong clearly and to punish and be punished for wrongdoing is part of a developmental stage and a part of most religions. Needs to evoke a righteous law and order; needs to be literal either in belief or disbelief; needs to make the individual the final authority, to rework and make old symbols richly meaningful, to reincorporate the past— these are all descriptions which Fowler makes of particular stages of development in faith. They are part of religious endeavor and practice in our society and in the churches we find around us.

No matter at what "level" of faith development we might be, the earlier levels reside within us and can be evoked by rituals and sensual stimuli. Our sermons and rituals can evoke different levels. A Jim Jones could speak to the child's need for dependency and for a clear sense of good and evil, reward and punishment—needs which lie within us all. It is not only the followers of a Jim Jones, however, for whom these issues are important. The trend in public opinion in favor of capital punishment shows how easily the punitive stages can come to the surface.

Perhaps you have been surprised by the reaction of a congregation to a sermon. I once preached a sermon in an unfamiliar church to which the entire congregation reacted with anger. I am still not sure why. That had surely not been my intention. Perhaps I was perceived as a punishing parent or had unknowingly devalued an authority figure who was important to that congregation. I may have left those people out of the salvation which I offered or separated myself from them, appearing to judge them rather than to be a part of the community of "sinners." By understanding the many-layered aspects of faith development, we can try to be more effective when we seek to change people with our words.

In the story, then, we give examples which ground our abstraction in the real world and our hearers learn and change as the images of the story affect and change our own images. For all of its identification with the "real world," the story itself is an abstraction. We need abstractions to allow us to experiment with behavior in our imaginations before we put that behavior into practice in our lives.

The advantage of this is explored by Piaget who observes that young children do not think abstractly. So a child who throws a rock through a window will not have the advantage of asking herself, "What will happen if I throw this rock through the window?" The consequences of the action—shattered glass, lovely tinkling sounds and new designs, followed by angry adult voices and possible physical abuse—cannot be thought through ahead of time. The available abstractions and images are often limited, even for adults.

In a comic strip encounter Lucy says to Charlie Brown, "There are two kinds of people, Charlie Brown—those people on a cruise ship who face their deck chairs to the stern to see where they've been and those who face their chairs to the bow to see where they are going. On the great cruise ship of life, Charlie Brown, which kind of person are you?" Charlie Brown answers in his usual modest tone, "I can't get mine unfolded."

Thank God for the Charlie Browns who have another choice in life rather than the either-or with which Lucy always faces us. We are out of the Garden of Eden where the choices were only to obey or disobey, to choose good or evil. It is in this broadening of choice that the greatest possibility of change takes place. We help in our sermons to broaden choices.

A Breadth of Choice

In her book, They Lived Happily Ever After,[7] Leslie Cameron-Bandler discusses the various ways in which people narrow their ability to choose. She uses the image of road maps. We all form road maps of our experience in our minds. We too often forget that the road map is not the road. The maps are extremely helpful but, as any traveler knows, the squiggly lines on the paper do not look like the streets of Boston. We need the abstractions to help us find our way, but we must be careful about confusing the abstraction with the reality.

Cameron-Bandler mentions three kinds of abstractions which we use to form our road maps but which may become too restrictive. In developing sermons to change people, we can remember these potential restrictions in our own road maps and in those of others.

The first abstraction which we need but which can become constricting is *generalization.* The generalization of God as a loving father

62

who demonstrates his love through the events of history may be a positive generalization about meaning and the texture of reality until you are caught in the Holocaust. Pastoral images for God made sense in a pastoral way of life but in an urban setting they may lack meaning and power. A male deity may give power in a society where male hierarchy is the only source of power but may be a false generalization for women seeking to be effective in shaping new relationships of power.

A second way we may limit our world is by *deletion*. We must continually delete experiences, perceptions, ideas and emotions in order to exist. If you had not deleted many of the extraneous noises and impulses in this room today, you would not have been able to have heard anything I said. If I had not deleted many thoughts and side-tracks in preparation of this paper, we would be here all day. Yet to delete the awareness of physical pain which warns of treatable health hazard may cause us to die earlier than necessary. To delete the awareness of discomfort and restlessness in the audience to which you are speaking may be to fail to communicate adequately. Our sermons can bring back things which we have deleted from our awareness: those we want to forget, such as injustice, misery or pain, and those we have forgotten in the work of everyday survival, such as joy, mystery and the numinuous. The sermon is the re-membering of a group of people, re-telling them who they are and how they could see, hear, taste and feel their world.

The third way we limit our world is by *distortion*. Every great dream or plan requires distortion. Every theory distorts reality. We shape our world in ways we would like it to be in order to make it become that way. Sometimes the distortion is too great and we make our images grotesque. It is hard to build bridges if we don't measure the river's exact width. It is hard to build great dreams unless we expose the dream to the daylight of others' criticisms and response. Too much criticism, it is true, may kill a dream, but choking off criticism may grow a monster, as all totalitarian groups, religious or political, remind us.

One way to enhance distortion is to define abstractions with other abstractions. Many a preacher has only defined theological concepts with other theological concepts. If we describe the "freedom to be" by saying that it is "existential liberty" or "living by the grace of

63

God," we may lose the traveler completely. It is as though we tried to get from Chicago to Los Angeles by tracing the road map but never set foot in a car or drove it on a highway. What our people want to know is the shape and nature of the beast. Does alienation have stripes or claws? Does evil prowl at night or leap in the sun-bright afternoon? And how shall we recognize joy—by its colorful feathers? Is the perfume of grace sweet to smell and does love taste like a ripe strawberry?

Ultimately we change people by restructuring their stories, by broadening their abstractions with new understandings and by showing them new road maps. But perhaps what people come to church to find most of all is another reality, one quite different from the one they think they know. It is a reality which is time out of time, a place where all scenes are particularly vivid, where good and evil is clear but where the characters are more than their outward appearance, not easily identified by their clothes or the beauty of their faces.

Frederick Buechner writes a magically sermonic book on preaching, *Telling the Truth*,[8] in which he says that the good news we have to bring is sad news before it is glad news (something is wrong before something can be made right) and that it is ultimately a divine comedy which is fairy tale.

The divine comedy tells us that the yellow brick roads lead back to a transfigured Kansas; that frogs and princes are all the same but love will bring forth the prince; that time must include the time to find the golden ring, the patience to know the girl with the long hair; that kindness to the ragged old hag is the magic that unlocks all one's desires; that a loving smile of a beloved daughter is far more valuable than all the gold in Fort Knox.

We must be wizards of words because most of us have forgotten the simple magic into which we were born. We forget to see this most amazing day until we are about to die. We forget to taste the tang of spring, to touch the frozen icicle of winter, to hear the locust hum of summer or smell the crushed apples of fall.

The wizard who forgets that the *world* and all who dwell therein are indeed magical will find her cap turned into that of a dunce. The wizard who forgets the spell which turns pumpkins into coaches and

64

E.T.s into beloved friends will find his voice become the frog's croaking. And the wizard who sees only a vale of tears in this divine comedy should turn in the lizard's liver and crystal balls of the trade to await a new transformation!

THE PREACHER AS PROPHET:
Preaching and the
Corporate Dimension

Judith L. Hoehler

Perhaps the central dilemma which confronts the preacher as prophet is revealed in the subtitle of this essay. We who have chosen to become parish ministers and ministers of religious education have chosen to do so within a specific corporate dimension, that is, within a local Unitarian Universalist church or fellowship. We are not free, therefore, to function solely as prophets. Prophets are uncomfortable; prophets are disruptive; prophets are destructive of the status quo. But preachers in the local parish setting are not only called to prophesy; they are responsible, also, for the well-being of the specific institution which invests them with the privilege and authority to preach. In short, by whatever image we characterize the pastoral side of ministry — whether as the shepherd of a flock, as the Executive Secretary of a voluntary association, as the first among equals, specifically trained in the skills of religious leadership — we cannot lose sight of the fact that we are responsible for the well-being of that corporate institution known as the local society.

I contend that the minister who neglects either aspect in preaching — either the prophetic or the pastoral — courts disaster. For the minister who is a selfstyled "prophet," the disaster lies in broken churches. We are all familiar with those situations in which the preacher hones the same controversial axe Sunday after Sunday, having nothing to do during the week with those who disagree with the prophetic message. One colleague during the anti-war movement told me that a delegation from the congregation approached after one service and said, in effect: "We basically agree with what you say, but do you think you might preach on topics other than Southeast Asia once in awhile?" And so, my colleague gleefully confided, "I preached the next three Sundays on Vietnam." By the time this minister was asked to resign, the congregation had been fractured almost beyond repair.

The minister who neglects the prophetic role, however, courts a different disaster. For the preacher who functions solely as a pastor, that result is not broken churches but churches which, at best, are irrelevant to the affairs of the world and, at worst, create oases of false peace and therefore function as bastions of support for the status quo, regardless of how unjust that status quo may be. It is the prophet who compels the church to be true to its mission as an agent of healing for *all* the world not just for those within its doors.

I remember when the Quaker philosopher, Elton Trueblood, came to my college campus years ago. He made what was for me a startling analogy. "The family," he said, "can be the finest incarnation of human love; but it can also be the most demonic." The critical difference is whether or not the family is devoted to a good beyond itself. If the welfare of the family is put above all else, you may have individuals practicing compassion and self-sacrifice within the family but you have unleashed a ruthless structure in society. If, however, family members understand compassion, mercy, justice to be God's will for the *whole* created order, their love spills over from the intimacy of family life where it is first experienced and practiced into the wider community beyond. In church life it is the prophetic voice — whether lay or clergy — which attacks every tendency to slip into what Trueblood has called the demonic incarnation of love.

I think no tension is more difficult in the life of a minister than that between prophet and pastor. All other roles in ministry — teacher, priest, organizer, community activist, counselor — contain stresses too but often these stresses are directly related to whether the moment calls for condemnation or comfort, challenge or support, judgment or acceptance, prophet or pastor.

In the chapter on "The Use of Symbols" in his book, *On Being Human Religiously*, James Luther Adams paraphrases Pascal in a way that addresses this topic. "According to Pascal," writes Adams, "the Christian has the obligation to exhibit opposite virtues and to occupy the distance between them. That is, we confront the obligation to pursue simultaneously the opposite virtues of freedom and order, freedom and equality, participation and privacy, and justice and mercy."[1] I would add: the preacher has the obligation to pursue simultaneously the opposite virtues of prophet and pastor...and to occupy the distance between them.

It might be helpful at this point to ask what a prophet is because I think that one of the reasons we have such difficulty in combining our roles of prophet and pastor is that we have bought into the 19th century romantic picture of the prophet as a rugged individualist, close to God in the kind of immediate religious experience of which Emerson spoke in his Divinity School address when he admonished his hearers with these now famous words: "Yourself a newborn bard

70

of the Holy Ghost, — cast behind you all conformity, and acquaint men (sic) first hand with Deity." We picture the prophets as iconoclasts, as religious geniuses who scorned the doctrinal beliefs and cultic practices of their tradition and who, through "acquainting themselves first hand with Deity," rose above the misguided mediocrity of the majority to pronounce stinging rebukes against injustice, ignorance and ritual practice.

It was only natural that this was the way the prophets would be viewed for this was the temper of the times in the 19th century, and era of "spiritual independence," "religious immediacy" and "social reform."[2] And it was in the 19th century that biblical studies had matured to the point (as a result of the advances of source criticism) that the prophets could be discovered as the remarkable group phenomenon they were. Up until the mid-1800s Protestantism had viewed the prophets as interpreters of the Law of Moses. They were seen as standing in organic progression from the Pentateuch which preceded them in the Scriptures. As the biblical scholar Gerhard von Rad has pointed out, "It was possible to approach the prophets in a new way as soon as the results of source criticism made it no longer necessary to assume that they were acquainted with the later...traditions of the Pentateuch. All at once the prophets emerged from the shadows which had obscured their real significance."[3]

Since this "emergence from the shadows" took place in the 19th century, it was only natural that scholars and laypeople alike should attribute characteristics from their own ethos to the prophets. Now, however, over one hundred years later, a more balanced perspective is being brought to bear on the prophets by contemporary biblical studies. Scholars have shown that the prophets were much more tied into the thought patterns and belief systems of the ancient Near East than had previously been supposed. Nor was this involvement only incidental; rather it wove itself through the very warp and woof of prophetic preaching.

"Now," as von Rad notes, "once this is granted, any definition of the prophet as a brilliant religious personality, standing close to God, falls to the ground. So, too, does the whole concept of 'prophetic religion,' which was set up as a spiritual counter-balance to 'the priestly religion of the cult.' "[4]

Modern scholarship is not out to debunk the prophets. Quite the contrary. Those men and women who emerged on the scene in the 8th, 7th and 6th centuries B.C.E. represent a remarkable flowering of incisive thought and religious inspiration at a time when Israel was on the verge of expiring. The new assessment does not downplay the extraordinary quality of the prophetic movement in Judaism. What it does is shed new light on what it was that made prophetic preaching so powerful. Perhaps a brief look at some aspects of that scholarship will assist our own attempts to become effective prophets.

What Is a Prophet?

Rabbi David Goldberg, in his book *Meet the Prophets*, calls them "spokesmen for God."[5] Since his book deals with the major prophets recorded in Scripture, we can perhaps forgive his use of the term "spokesmen" in this context. Actually, women, too, were prophets in Israel.

When one applies Old Testament scholar Phyllis Trible's principle of "depatriarchalizing" to the Bible [6] — similar to the process of "demythologizing" which many of us first encountered in seminary — when one attempts to break through the partiarchal mold in which much of the Old and New Testaments are cast, one finds ample evidence of prophetic activity by women. Indeed, two are named during the prophetic period: Huldah, who played a significant role during the reign of Josiah in the latter part of the 7th century, and Noadiah, who is briefly mentioned as the only one of the prophets who opposed Nehemiah. Miriam, the sister of Moses, and Deborah, the Judge, from earlier periods in Israel's history, are later referred to as "prophetesses."[7] So I think it is altogether accurate for us to rephrase Rabbi Goldberg's definition to say that a prophet is a "spokesperson for God."

But what does this phrase say to us? One thing it suggests is that the prophet's allegiance is not culture-bound; that is to say, those people who identify an individual as a prophet recognize him or her as having a transcendent source of authority. The prophet, therefore, has a freedom to speak that is not circumscribed by the need for conformity, for acceptance, for agreement by peers.

72

When we look at the historical setting out of which prophecy arose, we see that this radical freedom has always been a constitutive element in the prophet's relationship to the world. The prophets emerge in ancient Israel at that point when leadership — hitherto seen to have been exercised by God directly through empowering various individuals — is institutionalized in the monarchy. Before the era of the kings, charismatic tribal leaders arose as the times demanded: figures like Abraham, Moses, Miriam; and, in the period of the Judges, leaders like Joshua, Deborah, Gideon. From the human perspective, there was no rhyme nor reason as to who emerged as a leader in any given situation; the divine charisma — the spirit of Yahweh — lighted on whomever God chose. With the establishment of the monarchy in the 11th century, however, leadership became determined by human lineage.

> No matter how great the king's political power, the prophet as God's spokes[person] was always at hand to say "Thus says the Lord" to any king or to the people as a whole when they went contrary to the conditions established in the . . . Mosaic covenant. As a result, there could be no real curb on freedom of speech in ancient Israel.[8]

In his essay on "The Theological Bases of Social Action,"[9] James Luther Adams observes that this "freedom of the prophet presupposed a separation of powers which in a narrow way bears comparison to the modern ideal of freedom of the press." That is to say, prophecy flourishes only when space is allowed for freedom of speech.

When we look around at our local UU societies, we find that this very condition conducive to prophecy — the condition of freedom of expression — is structured into our polity. The most notable example is our hallowed tradition of "the free pulpit." We cannot underestimate the importance of this institution in our church life. I remember in the early days of the civil rights movement when, following the murder of Unitarian Universalist minister James Reeb, the call went out from denominational headquarters for clergy to join the march in Selma. My husband notified the chairperson of the Standing Committee, which was our governing board, that he would be leaving for Alabama on the following Monday and that his sermon the day before would outline why he was going. That week the parsonage was besieged with calls and visitors asking that he not go. Fearing a split in the congregation, the Standing Committee met early on Sunday morning. By the time of the service (which, need-less to say, was standing room only), the Standing Committee had prepared and distributed to the congregation a statement to the effect that, while individual members of the Committee might dis-agree that the minister's action was an appropriate one at this time, the Committee was unanimous in reaffirming the historic freedom of Weston's pulpit. The statement went on to say that the Committee viewed Harry's going to Selma as simply putting into practice what he preached from the pulpit. Therefore, they said, we wish to declare publicly that in his exercise of the freedom of the pulpit and in his exercise of the resultant right to follow his own conscience and act upon what he preaches, the minister enjoys our unanimous support.

As children of the Left Wing of the Reformation, with its radical emphasis on the freedom of the Holy Spirit, we Unitarian Univer-salists have built into our very church structure the space for expression which Adams and Wright have demonstrated is a necessary precondition for prophetic preaching.

The existence of such space in no way insures that the prophet's life will be an easy one. In fact, history teaches us quite the opposite. The lives of the Hebrew prophets were filled with danger, torment suffering, death. By the time of the New Testament, Jesus's words of comfort to the afflicted that "so persecuted they the prophets which were before you" illustrate the commonly held view in Israel of the fate of the prophet. Nor does that fate seem to change. John the Baptist was beheaded; Jesus was crucified; and, jumping twenty centuries to our own era, Martin Luther King was assassinated; Bishop Romero of El Salvador murdered.

Perhaps this persecution gives us a clue to the true prophet for, just as the creation of the space for freedom of speech does not promise an easy road for the prophet, neither does the existence of such space insure that it will be filled with truth. The Bible refers frequently to "false prophets," to those "who cry peace when there is no peace."

74

What, then, are the marks of a true prophet? To what dynamics do we need to pay attention if we would validate the prophetic dimension of our preaching?

The Marks of the Prophet

In his book, *The Message of the Prophets*, Gerhard von Rad, one of the greatest Old Testament scholars of our time, delineates three characteristics which might might be instructive for us. Von Rad believes that, despite the variety of expressive forms which each prophet uses; despite the very marked differences in the content of each prophet's message; despite the distinctive and unique circumstances of each prophet's life; despite the different concrete historical situations each prophet addresses; despite all these differences that must be kept in mind whenever we compare one prophet to another, there are three common factors which cut across the multiplicity and variety of the prophetic witness.

The first is that all the prophets are tied into their religious past. It is the sacral traditions of Israel which inform their messages. It is not their own individual truths, received through their firsthand acquaintance with Deity, which emerge in prophetic expression. Rather, their messages are drenched in the old traditions of the election of Israel and her covenantal relationship with God.

The prophets *do* exercise a great deal of latitude in this matter. Not only are they selective of those parts of the tradition from which they draw but they also re-work the tradition in innovative and often radical ways. Nor do they necessarily draw from the same ancient themes. Hosea, for example, "takes his stand on the old Israel-Covenant tradition" (von Rad), while his contemporary, Isaiah, never mentions it but rather turns exclusively to the Davidic tradition. The first similarity, then, which all the prophets share is a rootedness in their salvation history.

The second characteristic cutting across the various configurations of prophetic preaching is an intense interest in the future. The prophets read the signs of the times in light of what God was planning for Israel in the future. They interpreted world politics, with its calamitous consequences, first for the Northern Kingdom and then for the Southern Kingdom, as heralding Israel's coming

75

confrontation with God. Because Israel had broken the covenant, she would be destroyed but, although Israel had been faithless, God was faithful; Yahweh would address Israel with a new word, with new saving acts, in the future. The nature of these future events was informed by the historical tradition — that is, the prophets saw God acting in the future in ways that did not contradict past revelations — because it was, after all, the same God who was acting. The requirement of justice, for example, would be as binding in the new order as it had been under the old Covenant.

Rooted in the past, obsessed with the future, the prophets shared yet a third feature. That was their total immersion in the present. Each message was directed to a specific audience in a concrete situation in history. As von Rad puts it, "[I]t is all important not to read [the prophets'] message as if it consisted of timeless ideas, but to understand it as the particular word relevant to a particular hour in history, which therefore cannot be replaced by any other word . . . [The prophets'] concern was to deliver a specific message from Yahweh to particular men and women who, without themselves being aware of it, stood in a special situation before god."[10]

The message usually took one of two affective modes: either of condemnation or of comfort. Over and over the prophets announced God's sentence of death upon the status quo but always in the name of a new beginning, a future relationship of shalom with God. As preachers, we no doubt have drawn frequently on the awesome words of judgment in Amos or the magnificent words of comfort in Isaiah. But both prophets contain opposite messages as well. Jesus' teachings are illustrative here for they are perhaps a more familiar illustration of the same double-edged sword.

As the Roman Catholic sociologist, Sister Marie Augusta Neal has observed, there are two messages in the Gospels: to the rich, the powerful, the selfsatisfied of his time, Jesus preaches the wrath and condemnation of God; to the poor, the powerless, the oppressed, his message is one of comfort and promise. All this is offered in the name of the Kingdom of God which not only is coming toward us in its fullness from the future but is even now breaking in upon us wherever justice and compassion — which are marks of the future Kingdom just as they were demands of the old Covenant — are practiced.

Briefly summarizing the points we ought keep in mind as we look at our own prophetic preaching, then:

(1) we might imagine the prophets as "spokespersons for God"; that is, they practiced a radical freedom of expression because they experienced their power as coming from beyond them and from beyond the authority granted them by their hearers;

(2) they drew heavily, albeit selectively, from their religious past;

(3) they did this in light of their vision of the future; and

(4) their words were directed to the specific, concrete historical situation in which they found themselves.

The Function of Prophetic Preaching

The function of prophetic preaching is to being about change. The ancient prophets railed against the sins of their people, foretold impending doom, called for repentance, all in order to change the injustice; the oppression of the poor, the widow, the outcast; the apostasy of Israel. The story of Jonah is a constant reminder of this function. The author ridicules the prophet whose preaching brings about the desired effect in Nineveh (namely, the repentance of the city) yet, when the Ninevites mend their ways and God spares them from the destruction Jonah has foretold, Jonah goes up on a hillside and sulks. He gets angry at God because God has made a liar of him. Jonah seems to have been more interested in being right than in being effective. I suspect the same was true of the colleague to whom I referred earlier. Sunday after Sunday of sermons on Vietnam may have satisfied the minister's need to be right but it did not move the congregation to effective action on the war. Rather, this practice diverted the congregation's energies to the more immediate need of institutional survival.

Does this mean that, in order to be effective prophets in the pulpit, we cannot preach anything that goes against the majority opinion in our congregation? Of course not; that's a contradiction in terms. Prophets down through the centuries have hardly been persecuted for being innocuous. What it does mean, though, is that

77

if we want to be effective — that is, if we want to marshall group support to bring about changes — we cannot neglect the pastoral dimension of our ministry. It is at this point that the crucial significance of the tension between the prophetic and the pastoral aspects of ministry reveals itself.

When I was in Divinity School, I had a course with George Buttrick who at that time was Preacher to the University but had been for many years Minister of the Madison Avenue Presbyterian Church, one of the great pulpits in New York City. He used to tell the story of a Unitarian minister in whose congregation sat an important industrialist. Sunday after Sunday this man was in his pew, even though the views espoused from the pulpit were frequently anathema to him. After one particularly disconcerting sermon, another member of the congregation approached the industrialist with the following question: "Why do you come so faithfully when you so often disagree with what the minister says?" "Ah," smiled the industrialist. "Let me tell you. About a year ago I was very depressed, on the verge of suicide. I went to see the minister, spent over an hour in the parsonage study, but, when I left, I was still intent on ending my life. It was early evening and I walked to the bridge over the river. As I prepared to mount the rail, I was aware that I was not alone. I turned and there was the minister, about 30 paces behind me. 'Go away,' I called. 'I don't want your company.'

'I'm not accompanying you,' the minister replied. 'I'm simply out for an evening stroll.' Angrily, I plunged deeper into the park. Seeing that I was still being followed, I turned back into the city. All night I walked the streets. Every time I turned around, there was the minister, a discreet distance behind me. Finally morning came. Exhaustion overtook me and the urge to kill myself left. Only when I put the key in my own door did the minister turn to go home. Let me tell you: whatever the minister wishes to preach about, I will listen." The first step in effecting change is to maintain a climate in which one can be heard, in which one's words will be taken seriously.

But as prophetic preachers, we want not only to be heard; we want to empower the congregation to act for justice in a specific situation. Therefore there has to be ample opportunity for the people to talk back to the "prophet." We never preach a controversial sermon in Weston that is not followed by a "Sermon Talkback" after the worship service. The preacher is always present because it is the time for the preacher's hearers to air their views, to ask for clarification, to engage the preacher in discussion. In addition to "Talkbacks," we have forums, structured and run by laypeople, often with outside experts, to explore the issue yet again. And then there are those long, one-on-one visits with dissident parishioners. These latter conversations are extraordinarily fruitful for minister and layperson alike. They seldom lead to agreement but they clarify the thinking of both parties and more often than not mitigate against irreparable breaches. Finally, there are task forces. When it is impossible to reach consensus so that the church as a whole move to effect change, those interested in a specific issue form a task force which acts either on behalf of the church or on behalf of itself as a task force of the church.

These are a few strategies that supplement the function of prophetic preaching but no strategy removes the risk completely when an unpopular stand is taken. It was not for nothing that "so persecuted they the prophets which were before you." I can think of few controversial actions taken in Weston over the past fifteen years in which several people did not leave the church, at least temporarily. Nonetheless it remains true that the quality of our pastoral ministry has direct bearing on our ability to fulfill the function of prophetic preaching, the effecting of change.

The Structure of Prophetic Preaching

But it is not change for the sake of change that we are talking about in prophetic preaching. It is not even change for the sake of social reform, although that may be a byproduct. As James Luther Adams reminds us, "Prophetic religion speaks out of a religious vision; it is not first and foremost a movement of social reform."[11] Adams' statement underlies the importance of a self-conscious theology of the church. And that brings us to our second topic: the structure of prophetic preaching.

Religion is not solely rational. It is not irrational but it is grounded in myth and symbol structures that incorporate as well as transcend reason. Like the prophets before us, we cannot escape our past but we are selective about what experiences, what events, what truths from our past carry meaning for our lives in the present and shape our vision of the future. In the corporate dimension of our lives as preacher/prophet — that is, in the local society — the same dynamic is at work. Each church or fellowship shares a commonly owned history which sometimes consciously, often unconsciously, illumines the present behavior of its members. Prophetic preaching calls a people back to basically held beliefs and shows how these beliefs are not being lived up to.

Much of the power of prophetic preaching lies in the fact that it damns in the name of commonly held religious presuppositions. I believe feminist theologian Rosemary Ruether is right when, in her book, *Disputed Questions,* she writes: "Liberation theology has to criticize many of the emphases in traditional theology, such as individualism, other-worldliness, the divorce of the spiritual from the social, the imaging of God and Christ as white, male, ruling-class persons. These are not merely intellectual errors but sins of idolatry and blasphemy."[12] In other words, the prophet criticizes present behavior because it distorts, perverts what a group holds as fundamental religious truth. The prophet attacks present practice not merely as an intellectual error, not on the level of new truth supplanting old ignorance. Rather, the prophet attacks present unjust practice as idolatry, as blasphemy, as perversion of the fundamental truth commonly professed by a gathered religious community.

In harkening back to the election tradition, the prophets of Israel were condemning the glaring social evils of their times as a violation of the ancient Covenant with Yahweh. The sermon I preached in Rockefeller Chapel yesterday was first crafted for my congregation in Weston, a parish which considers itself a liberal Christian church. In the sermon I attempted to demonstrate that the feminist critique of male chauvinism is rooted in the very stories and symbol structure of the Christian faith and that faith calls us — nay, requires us — to expunge from our social structures sexism and all "isms" that oppress as we work for the realization of that future time when there no longer shall be diversions between "Jew and Greek, slave and free, male and female" (Galatians 3:28).

80

Were I a religious humanist rather than a Unitarian Universalist Christian, the content, the significant examples and presuppositions expressed in the sermon, would have been different but the structure of the sermon would have been the same. Effective prophetic preaching judges its hearers for present evils based on their religious tradition and in light of a future vision. The nature of that future vision depends on how the prophet interprets both the past tradition and his or her present experience.

If this analysis of the structure of prophetic preaching has any validity, it suggests that a major portion of our intellectual wrestling as preachers needs to be done with the religious heritage which informs our particular societies. In short, we need to do a lot of work in articulating for ourselves (and in helping our parishioners articulate) those basic assumptions which bind them together as a religious institution. Any effective prophetic preaching is rooted in what we affirm and celebrate as true. To put it another way, there is no true prophet who is not also a theologian, for a prophet calls the people to judgment based on the demands of their religious covenant. How a prophet does that leads me to the final topic.

The Ingredients of Prophetic Preaching

I have deliberately avoided the word "content" in this context because the content of our preaching will vary according to the specific concrete situation we are addressing and according to our faith stance. If prophets are "spokespersons" for God, the content of our sermons will be determined by the nature of the God we serve. We will be heeded to the extent that our hearers perceive our God to be true or false.

Webster's *New International Dictionary* defines content as "substance" and ingredient as a "component part." It is in this latter sense, as "component part," that I would now like to look at those ingredients which I believe are essential for effective prophetic preaching. These ingredients apply, regardless of the content of the preaching. They are (1) clarity of expression, (2) honesty of thought, and (3) knowledge.

81

Biblical scholar G. Ernest Wright points out that

> [o]ne of the most remarkable things about [the prophets] is the style in which they chose to deliver their messages about the meaning of current events. That style is a very elevated, carefully composed, and often beautiful poetry. This combination of message and poetic style is a most unusual and interesting feature of the classical prophets of Israel. The inspiration which they received from God did not result in the type of estatic utterance that characterized so many of the false prophets of their day; instead the inspiration led them to speak more beautifully and intelligibly than they otherwise would have done. These poetic works are products of careful composition and, as a result, have a great power within them that speaks not only to the emotions but to the mind. [13]

In other words the prophets poured enormous energy into crafting their utterances so that they not only could capture the attention of their hearers but so that their hearers would be quite clear about what the prophets meant.

To do this, von Rad points out, the prophets used a rich profusion of literary devices. Not only did they employ the traditional messenger formula — that is, "I come with the Word of the Lord" — and oracles against foreign nations, but also the prophets engaged in large-scales allegories, a theological discourse in Ezekiel, a pastoral letter in Jeremiah, "dialogues of the prophet with God, long soliloquies of lament," and so forth. [14]

Take the picture of the Valley of Dry Bones in Ezekiel. What more graphic way to portray God's destruction of the faithless Israel! Yet this picture of holocaust carries the promise also, for, in the words of the spiritual, "Dem bones gonna rise again." God will reconstitute Israel; this Israel will be faithful to God's ordinances of justice; and, concluded Ezekiel, "Then the nations will know that I the Lord sanctify Israel, when my sanctuary is in the midst of them forevermore" (Ezekiel 37:27). Surely Ezekiel's listeners got a clear message of God's destruction and re-creation from such graphic imagery.

Nor did the prophets restrict their clarity of expression to speech. Hosea married a harlot to illustrate Yahweh's faithfulness to an

Israel whoring after foreign gods. Isaiah walked naked through the streets of Jerusalem for three years to demonstrate the futility of Israel's alliances with Egypt and Ethiopia against the Assyrians. Jeremiah sported a wooden yoke for some time to prophesy Judah's submission to the Chaldeans. Whether by action or spoken words, the prophets went to great lengths to make clear their messages.

It is no easier for us. Clarity of thought requires work, the hard work necessary to discover or develop fresh language that causes listeners to say, "Aha!"

The most seductive trap for prophetic preachers is slogans. Slogans have a ring to them. They are easy to slip into. But rather than illuminate an issue, slogans cloud clarity of thought. Take for example, the slogans used in one of today's pressing moral issues: abortion. Those who support abortion often define themselves as "pro-choice." The use of this slogan allows us to focus on the decision of the woman as to whether or not she wants to have a baby; simultaneously, it allows us to forget about the fact that we are talking about aborting a human fetus. Similarly, those who oppose abortion often label themselves as fighting for "the right to life." This slogan allows us to focus on the admirable goal of protecting innocent life; it simultaneously insulates us from considering the injustices perpetrated against the poor who not only cannot afford the abortion clinics available to the rich but also who can least afford the burden of another mouth to feed. By casting the debate in the slogans of "pro-choice" versus "the right to life," we have obscured the real issue of abortion: that is, under what conditions and by whom is it permissible to take human life?

Paulo Freire, in his classic work, *Pedagogy of the Oppressed,* lays bare both the danger and the bankruptcy of using slogans in the struggle for human liberation. Slogans, he points out, treat your hearers as "things." Slogans do not engage people in dialogue with each other or with their own experience. And until this kind of dynamic takes place — what Freire (and thinkers coming after him) refer to as "praxis"; that is, reflection upon reality which produces action which in turn produces reflection upon that action, leading to more action/reflection — until this kind of dynamic takes place, no amount of prophetic preaching will bring about change. What Freire

83

says about the revolutionary teacher can be equally applied to the prophetic preacher:

> They cannot sloganize the people but must enter into dialogue with them so that the people's empirical knowledge of reality, nourished by the [prophet's] critical knowledge, gradually becomes transformed into knowledge of the causes of [that] reality.[15]

Slogans obscure reality; they do not lead to clarity of expression.

But the fresh language which is required for clarity of thought cannot be wrought without a second ingredient of prophetic preaching: honesty of thought.

I used to think, when I first learned how many hours good preachers put into writing their sermons, that the bulk of this time was spent in searching out pithy illustrations and polishing an elegant turn of phrase. I now know that by far the largest segment of time in sermon preparation is spent in agonized wrestling with the subject of the sermon. This is why we cannot preach someone else's sermon. Sometimes a layperson, on learning how much time goes into sermon preparation, will say sympathetically, "But there are books of sermons by great preachers. Why not just use one of those next Sunday?" But if a prophet is a spokesperson for God, *he* or *she* is that spokesperson. S/he cannot avoid the struggle, the hard work, the courage to speak a genuinely original word, that is, a word from the core of her being.

A New Testament refrain about Jesus is instructive here. The evangelists record that frequently the crowds describe Jesus as "one who speaks, not as the scribes or Pharisees, but as one having authority." That is, it is not "book learning" that we preach — not other people's sermons, regardless of how good they are. The authority required of us by our congregations is the authority which comes from wrestling firsthand with the issues about which we preach.

But there is another dimension in the definition, "spokesperson for God," which is critical here. It's not just that *we* are the spokespersons, but also that we are the spokespersons for God. We initiate the words from our own being; we do not initiate the Word of which our words are but the vehicle of transmission. Another way of

84

saying this is that, as prophets, we are not the creators of truth; rather we are bearers, revealers, witnesses to the truth, which stands over against us and judges and redeems us jst as it does our hearers.

It is with this Truth with a capital "T" that our agonizing wrestling in sermon preparation takes place, as we struggle to bring our feeble words in line with the Living Word of Truth active in our times. And it is a hazardous and risky business, this wrestling with truth. Not infrequently I find the sermon preached on Sunday morning is not the sermon I had set out to write the week before. For truth is not a fixed dogma stuck "out there" somewhere which we can study in abstract detachment. Saving truth, redeeming truth, judging truth is an active, pulsating power undergirding our very lives. Truth is a power working itself out in the world which engages us as prophets in the struggle for righteousness, justice, understanding.

How we image truth depends upon our faith stance; that is to say, the content of our sermons will vary, determined by the religious tradition which informs us and our congregations. But regardless of the religious conviction out of which we speak, I contend that we cannot be effective prophets in the pulpit if our preaching lacks clarity of thought, honesty of thought and yet a third ingredient, knowledge.

Walter Burghardt, the Jesuit theologian and master preacher, tells in his book on homiletics the story of a conversation he had with the Baptist preacher, Dale Moody:

> A student in [Dr. Moody's] Spirit course at the Louisville seminary wasn't meeting the professor's expectations. So Dr. Moody called him in and...said: "Son, you're not doing all that well in my course on the Holy Spirit. You been studying?" "Dr. Moody," the young man replied, "I don't have to *study* about the Spirit; I'm *led* by the Spirit." "Son," Moody asked, "that Spirit ever lead you to the library? If He doesn't soon, you're in deep trouble."[16]

We've already focused on the importance of a profound knowledge of the religious tradition in which both preacher and congregation are grounded. And we have dwelt on the crucial aspect of pastoral ministry, whereby ministers garner knowledge about the

85

hopes and struggles of their people. There is yet a third area of knowledge essential to the preacher who would be an effective prophet and that is knowledge of the times in which we live. The classical prophets of Israel had a keen awareness of world events and a wide store of information about what was happening around them. We tend to cling to a simplistic picture of the prophets as wild-eyed men in hair shirts calling people to repentance in stentorian tones and predicting doom in monosyllabic phrases. But even a cursory glance at their writings and sermons show that the prophets were extraordinarily knowledgeable of events not only in Judah and Israel but in the international sphere as well. One cannot be an effective preacher/prophet today without also doing the necessary homework. How else can one make the prophetic word relevant to the present time?

In his slender volume on preaching, Bishop Armstrong of the Methodist Church, for many years senior minister of the Broadway Church in Indianapolis, reminds us that "Preaching is truth-telling. Truth-telling is based upon reality. And reality — now, as always — is hard to grasp and harder still to rightly interpret."[17] There is no substitute for the reading and study necessary to give us an accurate grasp of current affairs. Laziness in this department undercuts the effectiveness of our prophetic message.

A case in point: in my Christmas sermon this year, I made the statement that "one of the more pernicious forms of exclusivism today is called economic stratification. The rich get richer and the poor get poorer. The gap seems to be widening between the 'haves' and the 'have nots,' between those on the inside and those on the out." You all will recognize the slogan, "The rich get richer and the poor get poorer." It has such a good ring to it. I wanted something with a little zing at that point in the sermon and I slipped into the lazy fallacy of the slogan.

Furthermore, I elaborated — not based on any reading I had done but on an *ad hoc* interpretation of the slogan itself. I said that the gap is widening between the "haves" and "have nots." After the service, a parishioner, an economist who attends church regularly and not just on Christmas, said, "Judy, you're wrong about the gap widening between the rich and the poor — in this country, at any rate. I've been following this for several decades and the frustrating truth of the matter is that, even when the federal government was deeply involved in social programs, we could not change by very much that gap between the poor and the middle class. The size of the gap is roughly the same today as it has been for the past 20 to 30 years." The thrust of my Christmas message was undercut with this economist because of my sloppy scholarship in his field. When we damn, we need to be accurate in our condemnation. That is no easy task for, in the the words of the Apostle Paul, it is against "powers and principalities" that we contend.

When I accepted as the subtitle of this lecture the phrase, "The relationship of preaching to prophecy and the corporate dimension," I did so because I wanted to highlight the corporate dimension out of which we preach: the local society. But the phrase also highlights the dimensions to which we preach. The issues of justice, today as always, deal not only with personal morality; they deal with the morality of social structures. The prophet must contend with such corporate dimensions of society as the prison system, multinational corporations, and sovereign political states, to name but three structures woven into the fabric of contemporary life. The pressing issues of nuclear arms limitation, abortion, equal rights, ecology, cannot be addressed solely as personal decisions; rather they are structured into how we behave as a society. Such issues cannot be simplistically addressed; we need to muster all the intellectual rigor, cultural knowledge and religious depth of the classical prophets if we would be prophet/preachers to our own age.

To fulfill the prophetic task effectively — to be "spokespersons for God" in the twenty-first century — requires that we understand and articulate the religious tradition out of which we come; that we judge the present moment in light of our religious hope for the future; and that we do this with clarity of expression, honesty of thought, and knowledge of our world.

Lest the task seem overwhelming, let me close with two words of encouragement. The first is a pastoral word of comfort from perhaps the greatest pastor of the second half of the twentieth century. When a reporter asked Mother Teresa of Calcutta if she did not become discouraged in her labors among the poor and dying, she replied: "God has not called me to be successful. God has called me to be faithful."

The second word of encouragement comes, fittingly enough, from one of the classical prophets. It is his vision of the future and I read it exactly as it has come down to us, with no editorial degenderizing. From the prophet Joel:

And it shall come to pass afterward,
    that I will pour out my spirit on all flesh;
Your sons and your daughters shall prophesy...

                                       (Joel 2:28)

THE EMPOWERING SERMON:
An Historical Perspective on Today's Unitarian Universalist Preaching

Irving R. Murray

For the pulpit is ever this earth's foremost part; all the rest comes in its rear; the pulpit leads the world. From thence it is the storm of God's quick wrath is first descried, and the bow must bear the earliest brunt. From thence it is that the God of breezes fair or foul is first invoked for favorable winds. Yes, the world's a ship on its passage out, and not a voyage complete; and the pulpit is its prow.[1]

Herman Melville, *Moby Dick*, 1851

A little more than a century after Melville wrote those lines, the journal called *The Pulpit* changed its name to *Christian Ministry* .

In 1876 Lyman Beecher Lecturer William M. Taylor said that the minister "must focus his whole heart and life upon the pulpit" and twenty years later in another lecture in the same Yale series, John Watson declared that "the most critical and influential event in the religious week is the sermon."[2] But in 1979 *Cleveland Press* pulpit critic George Plagenz, who reviews a church service each week, said that in two years he had heard only two sermons worthy of three stars (his Highest accolade). [3] Bishop Gerald Kennedy's definition of a sermon — something "a minister will not go across the street to hear but will go across the country to deliver" [4] — denigrates our collegiality and suggests that, even among the clergy, the sermon — at least, *anybody else's* sermon — is no longer what Watson thought.

This essay attempts to ring the changes in the image and the role of "the preacher" that these citations suggest; to inquire into the causes of these changes; and, more especially, both to assay Unitarian Universalist preaching today (as compared with the times of Frank Doan, Harold Marshall, Curtis W. Reese, John Haynes Holmes, and A. Powell Davies) and to essay the immediate future of the sermon in our liberal churches.

The American Preacher In History

The first newspaper continuously published in colonial America was the *Boston Newsletter* (1704-76). Its first edition appeared sixty-eight years *after* the prudent people of Boston, "dreading to leave an illiterate Ministry to the Churches, when our present Ministers shall lie in the dust,"[5] had established for themselves a college.

As late as 1790 there were only eight daily newspapers and seventy weeklies in the thirteen United States. The population of the new nation was almost four million, perhaps 45% of whom were illiterate.[6] The colonial preacher was in many cases the sole source of news in town and often for miles around. America had no acting company till 1749. Our oldest musical society was not established till 1761. The drama of the Christian year and the music of the church choir were the only public art accessible to most early Americans.

The Anglican Church was not separated from the state until 1777 in Virginia, New York, and North Carolina, 1789 in Georgia, and 1790 in South Carolina. It was not until 1818 that Connecticut disestablished the Congregational Church. Maryland waited until 1826 to drop its religious qualifications for voting and for public office.

Thus the theological foundation for the authority of the colonial American preacher was buttressed by cultural, social, and political realities. The preacher's position was virtually impregnable. There is no way that Jonathan Edwards could ever assert himself from any pulpit today as he did in Northampton, Massachusetts from 1727 to 1748. Edwards spent thirteen hours a day in his study and almost never visited his parishioners. He saw them only in the pew or in the casket. But even in the mid-eighteenth century there were limits to what a congregation would suffer at the hands of an authoritarian preacher. Edwards was dismissed in 1748 by a vote of 200 to 23.[7]

The spirit that would lead the American people to revolt against King George III was stirring. And yet the preacher who exercised any self-restraint at all then held a power over the people of that day far exceeding anything Americans would tolerate (or need) a century later.

The 1805-67 free public school movement empowered hundreds of thousands of Americans to make more of life, liberty, and the pursuit of happiness than their colonial ancestors had. As literacy increased, so did the number of newspapers. In 1860 there were 387 dailies as compared with eight seventy years before and 3,173 weeklies as compared with seventy — increases of over 4,500% for both, though the population was only eight times what it had been.

By 1860 there were opera houses in Boston, New York, and Philadelphia, and symphony orchestras in Boston, New York and Chicago. Chickering in Boston, Knabe in Baltimore, and Steinway in New York were making pianos. Americans could have music at home and in the concert hall as well as at church. In New York four theatres offered professional drama regularly by 1860 as did two in Boston. Not only in those two cities but in most of the country's more populous towns a dramatized *Uncle Tom's Cabin* and William W. Pratt's *Ten Nights in a Bar Room* rivalled the parsons of the 1850s in preaching abolitionism and temperance. The political warrant for the authority of the pulpit had been abolished and its cultural and social buttresses were now crumbling.

In the Western part of the country Methodist circuit riders continued to enjoy (if that is the word) some of the independence of earlier colonial divines. Peter Cartwright reported that the great mass of Western people "wanted a preacher that could mount a stump, a block, or old log, or stand in the bed of a wagon, and without note or manuscript, quote, expound, and apply the word of God to the hearts and consciences of the people." He ridiculed "young missionaries" who had "studied theology in some of the Eastern states, where they manufactured young preachers like they do lettuce in hot houses." Cartwright preferred the preacher who, "when he felt that God had called him to preach, instead of hunting up a college or Biblical institute, hunted up a hardy pony or a horse, and some travelling apparatus, and with his library always at hand, namely, Bible, Hymn Book, and Discipline," simply got on with the business of preaching the Gospel. [8]

Albert Barnes, Philadelphian, Presbyterian, a scholar, and a contemporary of Cartwright, held quite a different view of preaching. "Unless you can train your ministers to meet them [the infidelity and superstition Barnes perceived in some of the intellectual developments of his day] in the field where the freedom of mind is *contemplated* and let argument meet argument, and thought conflict with thought...you may abandon the hope that religion will set up its empire over the thinking men of this age." For Barnes, effective work in the ministry "demands...*all* the culture which can find mind to conflict with mind."[9]

Sidney Mead offers a model for understanding the history of preaching:

> The peculiar form and content of sermons in particular times and places have been determined by three factors. The first is the prevailing conception of the chief end of the ministry. Second is the status and role accorded to the minister by the society in which he is placed. Third is the immediate cultural context, since the minister in preaching has always, willy-nilly, felt the necessity to adapt himself somehow to the general level of interest and understanding of the people who sat in the pews.[10]

Cartwright's and Barnes' preachers were both evangelicals. The chief end of their ministries was to bring souls to Christ. The status and role accorded them by society remained one of dignity and prestige. But "the immediate cultural context" required of them a populist, "macho" style in the west and an academically correct and more comprehensive homiletical mode in Philadelphia. In Philadelphia a preacher who couldn't compete intellectually was lost, according to Barnes, whereas Cartwright required of Methodist circuit riders more physical than intellectual gifts.

The Philadelphia academic pulpiteer and the Western populist preacher were both, however, denied some of the theologically (and politically) based authority of the earlier colonial clergy. There had been in the eighteenth century more popular interest in what a preacher, trained in theology and the Gospel, had to say *qua* preacher. This interest was enforced by the establishment of religion and reinforced by the community's dependence upon clergy and church for news, knowledge, art, and even simple fellowship.

By 1860 urban men and women (at least) had other means wherewith to supply those needs. In the city pulpit, therefore, a preacher had to contend for attention which would have been given more freely a hundred years before.

Paradoxically, the social changes we have sketched brought forth a covey of preachers whom many call great: Henry Ward Beecher, Theodore Parker, and Phillips Brooks, to name but three. Beecher secularized the pulpit, even "religion itself [to] make it as common and universal as the air we breathe."[11] He cleared away the pulpit at

Plymouth Church in Brooklyn, replacing it with a kind of runway into and over the pews. The new arrangement brought him physically closer to the congregation and lent itself to a more dramatic presentation of his message. Gone was the high pulpit of the authoritative colonial preacher. Instead Beecher moved back and forth on the stage he had projected into the congregation, watching their faces to measure the command of his presence. When his brother Thomas substituted for him one Sunday, large numbers left the church as Thomas, rather than their idol, entered the chancel. Thomas sought to stem the tide by announcing: "All those who came here to worship Henry Ward Beecher may now withdraw — all who came to worship God may remain!"[12]

Phillips Brooks defined "real preaching" as "Truth through Personality." William Jewett Tucker declared that "the greater the personality of the preacher, the larger the use of his personality, the wider and deeper the response of men to truth," and B. B. Baxter, commenting on the changing conception of preaching in the minds of the Lyman Beecher Lecturers, noted that "The priest has not great demand for personality; with the preacher, however, such is not the case. More important than anything else is the man himself."[13]

Some of the practitioners of the "personality cult" were, indeed, preachers of power and pertinence — if you define "real preaching" as Brooks did. Theodore Parker is a notable example. His sermons addressed the major problems of his time and they resound with the trumpet call of prophecy. But preachers need always to remember that "we prophesy in part"...but only in part! For we are also priests, responsible for the care of souls and of a church. We are also responsible for *this* day as well as the far-off day of the Lord, "when nation shall not lift up sword against nation, neither shall they learn war any more." That kind of prophecy of course has its place in the liberal pulpit but a total politicization of the church follows upon the complete "prophetization" of ministry. The church itself becomes another battlefield, hardly a fulfillment of Isaiah's prophecy. Nothing like that of course befell Parker and his congregation. He preached every Sunday to hundreds of spellbound men and women. But within a year of his death, his church died too because it was *his* church--- really a Theodore Parker cult, in fact — rather than *a* church. [14]

95

A preacher, on the contrary, is charged to edify the congregation. The *achievement* of a fairer world requires the people's sustained, concerted energies, beyond all prophecy. Henry W. Bellows was right: "It calls for the organic, instituted, ritualized, impersonal, steady work of the Church."[15] Preaching that forgets this may stir the heart without getting the congregation to act to fulfill the word. We may — indeed, we must! — prophesy in part. But we cannot save the world every Sunday at 11:00 a.m. Some Sundays we must save the church.

Voices from the Early 20th Century

By 1977 United States and Canadian daily newspapers had attained a circulation of some seventy-seven million. The American election of 1944 forecast, nevertheless, the decline of their power. Thomas E. Dewey was supported for President by papers with 68.5% of total U.S. circulation; Franklin D. Roosevelt by less than half as many with only 11.7% of circulation. But Roosevelt defeated Dewey by some 3.5 million popular votes and by more than four to one in the Electoral College.

More pertinently, radio had come of age. In "fireside chats" from the White House (Teddy Roosevelt's "bully pulpit"), F.D.R. projected the image of an urbane, caring, wise father. Dewey, the *New Yorker* said, came across as a Lilliputian upstart who, worrying through the night in his sleeping car on the campaign trial, doubtless rose and walked off his worries, *under* the lower berth. It was radio more than any single factor that swayed the 1944 election.

Syncretism ("If you can't lick 'em, join 'em!") has long been the most facile mode of adaptation employed by social institutions and most notably by the religious establishment. Thus religious broadcasting was born. At its best it was a great experience for the American people. A radio voice which deeply influenced my generation in adolescence was that of Dr. Harry Emerson Fosdick (1878-1969). At the height of his powers, Fosdick had two graduate students employed full-time for him by Riverside Church to research every nook and cranny of human literature and present him at the beginning of each month with quotations, illustrations, anecdotes, and the like, a hundred times as many as he could possibly use in that month's scheduled addresses.

It was undoubtedly the G.I. Bill, offering World War II veterans the chance for a "free" college education that was the biggest single factor in the post-war growth of liberal churches. That, along with the demand for special skills by suddenly research-conscious industry, and the growing "service" sector of the economy, brought the U.S. to the point where (c. 1980) more than 25% of those Americans eighteen to twenty-four years old had attended one to three years of college. The increased numbers of men and women who had studied American literature meant more Americans were asking, "Emerson was a Unitarian, but what's that?"

The Manhattan Project (among other things, including some less ominous) had proven the value of scientific research to industry and government alike. The demand for physicists, biologists, and chemists meant that thousands more were brought to confront the conflicting testimonies of science and orthodox religion. Alienated from their former churches, many hundreds found a spiritual home in Unitarian Universalism. Thus we were brought to the "greening" of American religious liberalism.

It was a fortuitous blessing for Unitarian Universalist preaching. Nothing much new was required of us. Unitarian Universalist preachers of the period (as of the four decades preceding) proceeded much after the fashion of Channing, Emerson, and Parker. Our sermons took account of current biblical scholarship, Darwin, Freud, Marx, and (all too often) the newest passing fads, as well. Basically, however, we said what Channing might have, had he lived in this century, and we did so because we conceived of preaching essentially as he had: as an exercise of the free mind employed in the reconception of the meanings of religion in the light of advances in human knowledge.

The motif was similar to that described by Barnes but even more dynamic, more truly a genuine confrontation with "*all* the culture which can find mind to conflict with mind." Barnes expected "argument [to] meet argument" only to re-affirm evangelical orthodoxy. Unitarians and Universalists were prepared to abandon truth that time had made uncouth (to appropriate terms used by James Russell Lowell in "The Present Crisis"). Perhaps the best way to see all this

97

in practice is to sample some of the most notable preaching of the earlier part of this century.

A Potpourri of Preaching

Unitarian Frank C. Doan (1877-1927) declared his version of humanism in preaching in the 1920s on "Just Being Human":

> After all is said and done, after all the philosophy books have been read, after all the lectures and sermons about life have been taken in and digested, that is what we all are, is it not, — just human beings together? Perplexed, all of us, by the same human problems. All of us alike seeking for some light upon the path of this human life, — light and strength and wisdom and things like that. Divided against each other by the same human passions, greeds, envyings, animosities and things like that.
>
> Yes, but uplifted, all of us in our better moments, by the same human hopes, aspirations, dreams. Generous, all of us, at times almost to a fault. Affectionate, all of us, ready to die for those we love, ready to bestow all our goods to feed the poor, ready to give our bodies, if need be, to be burned, a willing sacrifice in any great cause of justice.
>
> In short, ready, all of us, and quick to respond to any and every appeal to our better impulses.[16]

Harold Marshall (1866-1932), ordained to the Universalist ministry in 1891, became manager of the Universalist Publishing House in 1917. In that post he worked to improve relations between church leaders and industry. The sermon from which an except follows, entitled "The Religion of Brotherhood," represents the distilled essence of his faith:

> The priests and the Levites are right in realizing that between their religions about Jesus and this religion of Jesus it is a duel to the death. Christianity as the way of life is another Samson loosed among the pillars on which ecclesiasticism and dogmatism rest. It is this rediscovery of Christianity as the way of life that makes sectarianism a spent force, morally impotent and spiritually sterile.

But discovery that stops with discovery is useless. Columbus might as well have found a cloud as a continent at the end of his voyage if adventure and agriculture and industry had not followed him. As we begin to explore this rediscovered religion of Jesus, we find it to be a religion of brotherhood (sic); that Christianity as the way of life means the way of brotherhood for all men, with all men. Love your enemy not because he is your enemy but because beneath his enmity is the eternal fact of brotherhood. Because there is one God and Father of us all, no child of God can be outside the pale of human brotherhood. [17]

Curtis W. Reese (1887-1961) was ordained a Baptist minister in 1918, but joined the Unitarians when convinced that his concern for labor and human problems would find a more congenial "home" with us. Here is an excerpt from his sermon, "The Faith of Humanism":

In his (sic) creation of spiritual values, man is hopeful and prophetic. Man achieves his spiritual values because he feels the need for them. He feels that he wants to secure more power in the pursuit of the good life. Hence, he has followed teachers who have proclaimed the more abundant life; he has made religions, and has evolved magic and prayer. Out of the inexhaustible soul of man, in response to his needs, have come forth gods and devils, angels and demons, heavens and hells. These man has made at his will and destroyed when he would. Other values innumerable has he brought out of the depths of his being, personified and sent them forth to battle in his behalf. These spiritual creations of man are so real that they die hard. Aye, they refuse to die until put to death by some greater spiritual creation.

But man's past achievements are only preparatory. They have merely opened his eyes to the greater possibilities of the future. In his power to dream dreams and to see visions, man is potentially the creator of nobler things yet to be.

Humanism holds that the religion that would be useful in this new day must be neither individualistic nor socialistic, but mutualistic. [18]

Of all my colleagues in my early years in the Unitarian ministry, none was more powerful than John Haynes Holmes (1879-1964) In his influence on American life, both within and outside the church. He has given us some of our finest hymns. His Community Church, New York, has set the pace for us in world-wide interfaith ecumenism. Holmes was one of the founders of the American Civil Liberties Union and a leader in that organization for the rest of his life. His fidelity to his scruples regarding international warfare inspired many thousands of young conscientious objectors. His close relationship with Gandhi helped to awaken American interest in India and its religions. Pacifist though he was, he was also a passionate fighter for social justice and it was this passion which he expressed in many of his sermons, notably in this excerpt from "What Does It Mean to Love God?":

> More important, however, than our relations with geographical space and cosmic space, are our relations with the men and women who populate this globe. Most of us are tribal creatures; we are interested only in those persons whom we can see and feel and know — the members of our family, the citizens of our town, our associates in business or in pleasure. The people who for any reason live beyond the borders of our experience, the multitudes whom we cannot or do not see and therefore do not know, to these we are usually as indifferent as we are on occasion hostile. We have not concern for the man (sic) who belongs to another social class, lives in another section of the city, or is a member of an alien race or nation. We have not imagination enough to understand the aspirations of these people, or to sympathize with their difficulties and sufferings. If we think of them at all, it is usually to fear them or hate them, because they live in a different manner, use a different language, are loyal to different principles and ideas, from ourselves.

> Every now and then, however, there appears a man whose human interests cannot be confined within the borders of his particular family or tribe. He loves men just because they are men . . .

> A man may be said to love God when he emancipates himself

from the bondage of past and present, and reaches forth into the future of a better world, and gives himself unstintingly not to the preservation of what has been and now is, but to the creation or fulfillment of what may and ought to be.[19]

Frederick May Eliot (1889-1958), President of the American Unitarian Association in the last twenty-one years of his life, was a preacher of commanding presence. This is an excerpt from his sermon in Harvard's Memorial Church the Sunday before Thanksgiving Day November 20, 1955:

The other illustration that I would use comes from our own tradition here, four lines by James Russell Lowell, lines which I had never discovered although I really thought I knew the writings of that one of our Cambridge boys. But I never read these lines. At least I have no recollection of ever having read them until a friend of mine in England last summer told me that he thought they were among the greatest words ever written! He said, "My critical friends tell me they're bad poetry, but," he said, "they are great words." You'll find them in a poem about Miles Standish. These are the four very simple lines.

He had stiff knees, the Puritan,
That were not good at bending.
The homespun dignity of man
He thought was worth defending.

Now the Puritan, for most of us today, I suppose, is rather an ungracious figure, austere, perhaps sublime, not very friendly.

But the Puritan really believes in the homespun dignity of man (sic) his own, yes; but much more than that, the dignity of all men. The homespun dignity of man: he believed in it and he thought it was worth defending. And he proceeded to defend it with might and main.

When he thanked God, the Puritan had that faith and that resolution in his heart, and he cleansed his heart of the selfishness that vitiates thanksgiving.

Whether it be in terms of the beauty of the world, or the moral imperative, or what one hears in conscience and that gives one

101

no rest until it has been obeyed, wherever it comes from, each
one of us must find somewhere the cleansing power that will
make it possible for him honestly, sincerely, genuinely and
self-forgettingly to join the universal chorus of praise, and to
say, "It is a good thing" — for me — "to give thanks unto
God."[20]

As the twentieth century wore on, the first person singular
pronoun was heard more and more frequently from the pulpit.

John Haynes Holmes himself could be quite subjective. Here is an
excerpt from a sermon he did in the form of "A Letter to Mahatma
Gandhi" on the Hindu leader's seventy-fifth birthday. Holmes had
begun by reporting that an essay on Gandhi by Gilbert Murray had
transformed his life. Next he recounted his earliest personal encounters with his patron saint. And then he confessed his faith:

> Above all, you have proved to me the practicability, the stu-
> pendous power of your ideals. I have talked with you about this
> before. I have seen it in the early Christians, in St. Francis, in
> Tolstoi. In 1915 I preached a series of sermons on non-resist-
> ance.

> But all this never really came alive until I knew you. At that
> moment I saw, as by a lightning flash, all that Jesus had meant by
> his Gospel of love. Then after the inital flash there came the
> wondrous flows of your exaple.

> I understood what Christianity, Hinduism, all true religions,
> must really do for men (sic) to save them and their world by the
> sheer power of the Spirit.

> Secondly, by teaching me the meaning of religion you showed
> me the way of life...[21]

One cannot be sure that Phillips Brooks would have endorsed the
gospel of Norman Vincent Peale (1898-). But Peale has certainly
embraced Brooks' notion of "real preaching" as "Truth through
Personality" — as shown, for example, in this excerpt from Peale's
sermon, "Exciting Living for Excited People," from the pulpit of the
Marble Collegiate Church, New York, sometime in 1978:

Two or three weeks ago I was scheduled to speak to the Ohio State Convention of Real Estate Operators, in Cincinnati. And the minister of the church there, the Grace United Methodist Church, hearing that we were going to be in the city, asked me would I preach in his church. (His name is Dr. Acup.)

And I was very glad to accept this invitation because, back in 1905-1910, my father was pastor of this church; and under his ministry it was the beautiful building that exists today that was erected. And at the time that this church was dedicated I was a very young boy. Just how young I am not about to tell you, but I was very young.

But not too young to remember! And I had my son, John, come up there, and my grandson, Charles Clifford Peale, named after my father — my wife was with me — and we had a kind of nostalgic time.

You all have a hometown, haven't you? Looking around here, Oklahoma City I see over there, down south from Tennessee I see another. Well, Cincinnati is my hometown. And when you go back to the hometown, you think of a lot of things. It's a good thing to do once in a while.

And I remember being a minister's son in that church. No wonder ministers' sons got such terrible reputations! I remember that my father was preaching a Fourth of July sermon; and my father was a great patriot. In fact this building has in it a replica of the dome of the statehouse in Columbus, Ohio. My father was once offered the nomination for Congress. But he wanted to be a minister. I think he had a secret yen to be Governor of the State because he had that dome built into the church. And he would, when he got fired up on a patriotic subject, he was really terrific! And he was laying it out on the Fourth of July, on a hot Sunday in July. And my brother Bob and I were very young. Bob was younger than I. We were on the outside and we had a what's-known-as a cannon-cracker — big noise! And just as my father brought his fist down on the Bible, off went the cannon-cracker. Now you'd think that any self-respecting father would apply manual punishment afterwards. But you know what he said? "I'm glad you made it synchronize!"

You see, my mother and father were *excited* people. And they told us this is a wonderful world. They loved beauty. They loved springtime, the glory of autumn, the snows of winter, the sky at night, with the everlasting stars, the forget-me-nots of the angels. And they tried to make their children excited people. They said it's a great, exciting privilege to live in this world, with the Lord and with other people. And you've been put into the most glorious country in the world. So be excited about it!

I remember the day at that church (and I sat there in the pulpit thinking about it) when I came up with some other kids to become what they called Preparatory Members of the Church. And my dear old father leaned down, and he said, "Listen, you kids. Jesus is the most exciting personality that ever lived. And if you want to live an exciting life you'll follow Jesus all the way. He will make it thrilling for you, and you will be able to overcome every difficulty you'll ever face in this life!"

I was impressed. And I thought to myself — *that* is wonderful! *That* is terrific.

Peale has outlived A. Powell Davies (1902-57) by far. Davies obviously directed his preaching to a more sophisticated segment of the public than Peale seeks to reach. Something akin to Peale's subjectivism is evident, nevertheless, in this excerpt from Davies' October 16, 1955 sermon on the "The Right to Disbelieve":

I remember that back in August, 1948, the Federal Communications Commission, relying on American founding principles, directed that broadcasting stations should sell time to atheists, if they wanted it, to argue the case for their disbelief. A certain Robert Harold Scott had tried to do this in California, but had been denied the right. So he petitioned the Federal Communications Commission to revoke the licenses of the broadcasting stations on the ground that they were allowing religious belief to be widely and freely disseminated from their studios, but they were not allowing any opportunity whatever for rebuttal.

He was a peaceful man, said Mr. Scott. He did not throw stones at church windows. He did not mock at people kneeling in prayer. He respected everyman's (sic) right to have and to express any religious belief whatsoever. But he abhorred and denounced those who, while asserting this right for themselves, sought in one way or another to prevent others from expressing contrary views.

The F.C.C. thought that Mr. Scott's position was eminently fair. No principle, said the Commission, is more embedded in our Constitution than that of religious freedom. And such a freedom necessarily carries with it freedom to disbelieve; and freedom of speech mean freedom to express disbeliefs as well as beliefs — which, if you understand the American Constitution at all, and believe in it, is transparently obvious. But it got the F.C.C. into trouble.

A special committee of Congress made an investigation and described the reasoning of the F.C.C. as dangerous and mischievous. It advised the Commisson to conform to the rules of orderly decency, and the sensibilities of a listening public. In other words, the Commission was told to ignore the founding principles of the Constitution, and to allow only what conventional and timid people wanted.

I remember that at the time this occurred, I defended the Constitution publicly, which caused a good many people to be a little surpised, not to say dismayed! They wrote me letters. Why would a minister protect the rights of an atheist? The implication of the American founding principles, that the rights of any are the rights of all, was entirely lost upon these people. You were supposed to defend only what you agreed with. And a minister, how could he defend an atheist? Surely his business is to defend his God! Which struck me and still strikes me as delightfully quaint.

What sort of god must it be who trembles in his heaven at the broadcast voice of an atheist?...[23]

Compare now, if you will, Davies' preaching with that of Archbishop Fulton J. Sheen, (1895-1979), heard in the following excerpt from his Good Friday, 1978 sermon on "Spectators: Where Are Your Scars?" at St. Agnes Church, New York City. Sheen has told a huge — and wildly applauding — congregation he is grateful to them for coming, and to God for permitting him to keep his fifty-eighth Good Friday as a priest:

> The grace of God worries you, and disturbs you! This came to light to me very recently, about a convert I made some years ago. That was Louis Budenz, formerly editor of the Communist *Daily Worker*. (He died just a few years ago.) I was talking to his widow, Mrs. Budenz, on the phone just the other day, and she recalled the first time that we met.
>
> Budenz, as the editor of the Communist *Daily Worker*, wrote to me, and said, "Will you take dinner with me?" It was rather embarassing. I had been writing articles against the Communists; and he had been writing in the *Daily Worker* against me. Not until the phone call last week from Mrs. Budenz, did I know that it was the head Polibureau (sic) of Russia that had ordered Budenz to have me to dinner. They felt I was doing too much harm to the cause; and since he was of the faith as a boy, they felt that he could approach me. But I didn't know that then.
>
> So when we sat down at the table, Budenz said, "Now I will tell you what we Communists have against you. You do not believe that Russia is a democracy." But I said, "How can it be a democracy, in the light of Article 125 of your Constitution?" He said, "What is Article 125?" "Well," I said, "as you see, I know your Constitution better than you do!" So I said, "We're not going to talk about it. I'm going to talk about your soul."
>
> Now this is the point of the words in *Spectatorship*. Not until this week did I learn that, when he went home that night, he said to his wife, "I was never so angry in my life! Here I was, sent by the Politbureau to talk Communism to this man, who knows it, and you know what he said to me, after he mentioned Article 125? He said, 'I'm not interested in your Communism. I want to talk to you about your soul.' Imagine! He said, 'My soul!' I'm not interest in that."
>
> From that point on, she told me, whenever I appeared in radio

(those of you who are over a hundred and two will remember that) — when I appeared nationally on radio, she said, he would become furious when my voice was heard in the house, and ordered that the machine be turned off. He said, "I can't stand to hear that man's voice!"

But Mrs. Budenz also said, "I was not a Catholic. I was a Communist. We were not married, just living together. But," she said, "do you know that every night, before we went to sleep, he would reach over and make the sign of the Cross on my forehead?" She said, "I never knew why he did that. I did not know what it was."

Seven years later I received a letter from him, asking to see me, about his soul. And she said, "Why are you writing to him, when you hate him so much?" And he said, "Because he talked to me about my soul." He said, "All this time I was worried, really troubled in spirit." And that's the way every spectator is in this church, who is fallen from grace, or in the state of sin, or needs reconciliation with God. We watch. We feel we do not believe, but we half-believe; and we carry with us maybe a few remembrances and relics like the sign of the Cross on the forehead at night.

But as spectators, the Lord will take us. Even when we are unable to walk, if you but stumble into those confessional boxes, He will welcome you back.[24]

On tape Sheen uses up five minutes and fifty-five seconds to preach the sixty-three lines above (as compared with Davies' three minutes and forty-five seconds for the fifty lines from his sermon preceding). Archie Worthing, a University of Pittsburgh teacher of physics, told me in 1945: "Murray, you should pause more often in preaching your sermons. Give me time to preach to myself." Sheen was a master of that.

Shortly after Worthing made that remark, Melvin Arnold, then Director of Publications for the American Unitarian Association, mailed our Unitarian clergy a research report on our preaching, based upon Rudolf Flesch's studies of word-lists a thirteen-year-old could be expected to understand. Flesch had counted the occur-

107

rence of these words in the texts of certain magazines of the day. *Life* was written so that a thirteen-year-old could easily comprehend almost 90% of its language; *Time* , 70%; *The Atlantic Monthly*, 30%. A random sample of Unitarian sermons showed them including only 18% words whose meaning you could expect the average junior-higher to know. In this context, please re-examine the excerpts from the last four sermons given above. Holmes and Davies scored better than most of us would on Flesch's scale, but certainly Peale and Sheen use an idiom any *Life* reader could understand — more than Holmes and Davies do.

I asked the UUA recently to send me, if they could, a copy of that report by Mel Arnold. After some time I received word that it could not be found. I thought, when I first received it some thirty-odd years ago, it was the most useful communication I'd ever had from our denominational headquarters. I still think that. And I think it *may* be characteristic of us that this important document is not only forgotten but lost, as well.

Every one of us knows that when Search Committees follow the Congregational Handbook in their quest for a new minister for their church, they begin by polling the congregation as to what they want of the next parson. Almost invariably congregations tell their Search Committees, "Find us a *preacher* !" But the Seminar for which this paper was originally prepared marked the first time in my forty-three years in our ministry that the denomination offered its clergy and theologs a major opportunity for in service training in preaching.

Powell Davies in thirteen years in Washington, D. C. brought about the establishment of seven new churches in the area. He did it as a *preacher* . A new respect for the role of preaching and the skills it requires may be the essential ingredient of the denomination's current growth efforts — an ingredient too long neglected, if not, incredible though it seems, ignored.[25]

A Survey of Current Preaching

We turn now to a consideration of Unitarian Universalist preaching today. A summary of my data-base will be found in Chart I. Here we encounter the first reference to women as preachers to be found in this essay.

CHART I

SUBJECT-MATTER OF SEVENTY-TWO SERMONS BY 30 UU CLERGY

1. FESTIVALS (Easter, Xmas, Flower Communion)	5
2. PRAYER & WORSHIP	4
3. GOD	5
4. THE CHURCH (Unitarian Universalists)	3
5. UNITARIAN UNIVERSALISM (History, Heroes, Problems)	10
6. COMPARATIVE STUDY OF RELIGIONS	3
7. SPIRITUALITY	1
8. "EPISTEMOLOGY" (Faith & Reason, Myth & Truth, etc.)	5
9. SOCIAL ACTION (Political)	5
	—
Subtotal	41
10. "How one meets death" (a)	1
11. "The meaning of tragedy"	12
12. "The nature of obligation" (b)	7
13. "The character of love" (c)	11
	—
Subtotal	31

(a) Daniel Bell, March, 1977, in the Hobhouse Memorial Lecture at The London School of Economics: "Religion is set of coherent answers to the core existential questions that confront every human group, the codification of these answers into a creedal form that has significance for its adherents, the celebration of rites which provide an emotional bond for those who participate, and the establishment of an institutional body to bring into congregation those who share the creed and the celebration and provide for the continuity of these rites from generation to generation." Categories 10 through 14 are based on Bell's four "core existential questions." As for categories 1 through 9, I have detected little "codification"; 1 and 2 certainly deal with "celebration"; 4, 5, and perhaps 7 refer to "institutional body."

Subjective judgments are of course involved in the categorization of these seventy-two sermons by subject matter. But with only five of them dealing with social-political action and, in the judgment of this reviewer, fifty-six of them squaring rather well (save for his emphasis on "codification") with Bell's definition of religion, is not Unitarian Universalist preaching, assuming the categorization is at least partly accurate, somewhat and perhaps quite different today from what it was forty years ago?

How was the sample chosen from which such a conclusion might be drawn? UUA Executive Vice President, William F. Schulz, at my request, chose forty of our colleagues who are recognized as among our outstanding preachers and asked them to send me two of their sermons which they considered representative of their preaching style and substance. The forty included twelve women, of whom ten sent me sermons.

(b)   There is some overlap here with 9 but no sermon has been counted twice.

(c) Some overlap with various sermons in 1 through 9; but no sermon has been counted twice and in every case I have categorized each sermon in terms of its dominant thrust.

It is not that there were no women clergy before now. There were a few but *very few* . In the nineteenth century, Universalism profited from the ministry of more women clergy (proportionally and very possibly in real numbers too) than any other religious body, the Unitarians *not* excepted. Today, moreover, the number of women holding and preparing for fellowship in the Unitarian Universalist ministry proportionately exceeds that of all other major U.S. and Canadian denominations.

The effects of this development are already far-reaching. Much of the best preaching in my "sample" (Chart I) is by women. Many of these women ministers appear (from the Directory statistics) to serve churches that called them as minister on the basis of their intrinsic merit, whereas in earlier decades the choice of a woman as minister sometimes betokened an austerity budget for a sexist congregation willing to "put up with her" to save money. Many women left the Unitarian and Universalist ministry late in the nineteenth and early in the twentieth centuries because they could not live on the wage of a woman minister in our churches. Even today, indeed, the salaries of most Unitarian Universalist women clergy fall below those of men but the trend is away from this economic discrimination. As preachers, the ten women included in my sample on the average excel the twenty-eight men and, as noted in Chart I, 5/6 of the women (as opposed to 9/14 of the men) responded to the request for sermons, evidence of more responsible participation by women clergy in a significant denominational undertaking than was shown by the men in the sample.

When I attended Harvard Divinity School, there were no women students. Today the majority of our theologs are women. It has made a great difference to a new generation of preachers that neither in school nor in their profession have they been separated from the opposite sex. It has made our younger male clergy more sensitive to important nuances of human behavior and communication (in its immediacy, as perceived without the filters of abstraction). And, at the risk of being judged still somewhat chauvinistic, I daresay it has helped women clergy better understand and participate in the abstract ideological bent of much male thought and feeling.

All these developments are reflected in many of the contemporary sermons read in the preparation of this essay. Today's feminist revolution — especially in our theological schools, but also in American life generally — is yielding a richer kind of preaching.[26] This is doubtless a major factor also in my judgment that the preaching included in my sample is better, more serviceable to the people in the pews, wiser, certainly more understanding of human nature, and oftentimes more spiritually fulfilling than that in the profession forty years ago, [27]

I found no Powell Davies in my sample, no John Haynes Holmes, no Fulton J. Sheen, and — thank God— no Norman Vincent Peale. But every one of my thirty preachers of today lives closer to his or her congregation than Davies and Holmes did. The Second Isaiah fulfilled the needs of *his* time quite as adequately as the first, historic

Isaiah did those of the earlier period in Israel's history. It *may* well be that a comforted people will beat their swords into ploughshares more readily than a people resentful of a prophet, resentful even though he is probably right and resentful exactly because he or she is beating their ears off!

This is *not* to say that today's Unitarian Universalist preaching ignores social evils and our responsibility for their remedy. Nothing of the kind! The assignment of sermons to the categories of "dominant thrust" in Chart I must not be misread as implying, for example, that in 92% of their preaching, today's Unitarian Universalist parsons ignore the need for religiously motivated social and political action. On the contrary, even though only five of the seventy-two sermons are predominantly activistic and political in their major thrust, virtually none of them overlooks the need for socio-economic change if life is to be more fulfilling.

It is twenty-two years since Beacon Press published *Contemporary Accents in Liberal Religion,* a volume of Unitarian Universalist poems and sermons edited by Bradford E. Gale. Thirteen years before that, we published *Voices of Liberalism,* a similar anthology, whose Preface expressed the hope it would be the first of an annual series of such volumes. A second *Voices of Liberalism* appeared in 1948. Then nothing until 1960. My reading of seventy-two sermons by today's Unitarian Universalist preachers was such a heartwarming experience that I find myself wishing many more might share it. Could we not find a hundred of us to secure the fulfillment of the hope of *Voice of Liberalism* (perhaps by underwriting the sale of at least twenty-five copies in each of our churches *each year* a new volume appears), to flesh out the faith, hope, and love of liberal religion among us, annually?

Self, Sermons, and Dialogue

How often have we found ourselves, draped in a decorous Geneva gown and self-imprisoned in the steel armour of the sermon style, envying the candor and audacity of David, "I cannot go with these; for I have not proved them, and David put them off." Would that we had the courage to slough off the traditional mannerisms of the pulpit and to do the natural thing in the natural way. Those five smooth stones which David took from the brook, familiar to the hand and proved in the sling, ought to be sufficient charter for informality even to this day.

We know well enough what we are trying to do. We are trying to save the sermon from dying by inches of a kind of literary arthritis. [28]

Dean Sperry (1882-1954) was, in this passage, discussing "The Cult of Unconventionality" in his Lyman Beecher Lectures. We have all known the yen to escape the confines of the pulpit. I have in passing, detailed how Holmes, Peale, Davies, and Sheen sometimes spoke overmuch of themselves. A sound convention encourages the faithful preacher to use the first person primarily in its plural form, rather than the singular. But, when we are put upon (or think we are) by an unappreciative congregation, it *is* tempting to remind them of how lucky they are to have in their pulpit a man or woman who hob-nobs with the great. And so some of our sermons become cluttered with gratuitous ego-in-flaters: "The last time I talked with Adlai Stevenson. . ." or "As Gloria Steinem said to me on the phone the other day ..." Such indulgences will do little harm if they occur infrequently. But if they recur again and again, it is best to take a Sunday or two off to restore your self-acceptance of what and who you are!

The first person singular may, indeed be used openly and freely in preaching, to establish your status in the pulpit as that of mortal, fallible human flesh and spirit, called upon to articulate, if possible, something of the grandeur and tragedy of, in Robert Browning's phrase, "infinite passion, and the pain of finite hearts that yearn." Such "confessional" preaching should of course avoid both the Scylla of self-inflation and the Charybdis of self-flagellation.

Elsewhere Sperry has cited an Anglican priest who declared, "In certain kinds of trouble no one can help as much as someone who says, 'I, too, have experienced that.' " In such case the first person singular is used only to affirm how much we share. In most of the seventy-two sermons in my sample, it has been so employed. These younger preachers are not *driven* to talk about themselves. Rarely do they forget that "I" am impossible by myself alone; I *am* only in the "I-thou" relationship. These younger preachers have learned that and made it a part of their selfhood (or "I-thou") and of their professional life and ethic. Henry Bellows would rejoice for his church, served today by a generation of preachers who do *not* scorn their priestly role in favor of an outmoded and mortally perilous individualism-for-individualism's sake.

Even so, the rest of what Sperry has to say about "The Cult of Unconventionality" is worth reviewing...

> The difficulty with the cult of unconventionality is this; when we are properly employed about the concerns which are committed to our charge we are dealing with a few constantly recurring experiences, ideas, emotions, purposes, and needs which man (*sic*) has always associated with religion. It would be irrelevant in the sermon to talk about the weather. Book reviews are a poor substitute. Our contributions to the political and economic wisdom of society are not uniformly important. But we are supposed to know something about the divine discontent which gnaws forever at the heart of man, making him a pilgrim and stranger on the earth. And we have to put these deep, constant, recurring concerns into words, and deal with them Sunday after Sunday. . .

> We might as well, then, begin and continue our preaching with the candid admission that sermons cannot be permanently unpatterned utterances. We are not under bonds to be slavishly subservient to old homiletic patterns, but we must recognize the inevitability of the principle of pattern. I end with a dogmatic statement which is worth what it is worth — most of man's beautiful and permanently enduring creations have been wrought within a pattern and in conscious consent to it, rather than in deliberate neglect of it. [29]

Our orthodox colleagues, meanwhile, have recently been subjected to incitation to novelty. Thus Clyde Reid, in his *The Empty Pulpit*, warns that "there are many signs that people do not hear preaching anymore, and particularly do not *hear* it in such a way as to influence their behavior at deep levels." And Reid concludes that "we cannot continue [preaching], as before."[30] Why? Reid holds that the electronic "revolution" has initiated a "new age" which has birthed a "new man." This "new man," according to Reid refuses to think as his parents did. "For him, truth is much more a matter of total awareness than clear, logical idea."[31] (If there is any such thing as "total awareness" outside of LSD-narcosis, can it be without "clear, logical ideas"?)

Reid follows this oversimplified, apocalyptic version of Marshall McLuhan's views with a statement of "a few of the implications of the 'new age' " even though he admits that peering through his crystal ball "is a risky business." Parts of this statement are worthy of consideration:

1. We must find means of communication that will reach people "through all the senses at once"... The repetition of words and abstractions from a pulpit on Sunday morning is not enough...

2. We must use a variety of methods to communicate to modern men and women, alternating our approach to reach them in different ways. To use the same rigid style of communication over and over, whether it be preaching or any other, is deadening.

3. Modern men and women will learn much more through actual experiences than through hearing speeches, logical propositions, or doctrinal formulations... We must learn to teach through involving them in action rather than talking at them when they have ceased to listen.

4. Modern men and women will be convinced more easily when our actions and deeds show a high correlation, when they do not contradict each other ...

5. Modern men and women are increasingly impatient with those structures in which they are only passive spectators..., They want to be regarded as partners rather than as dependent followers, and they desire an increasing share in the decision-making processes which affect their lives... Those communication structures which emphasize passive-dependent listening will continue to appeal to those who have strong needs to surrender their individuality to a parent-figure. Those person who have learned to trust their ability to think for themselves will be drawn to communication structure which honor their gifts — in or out of the church.[32]

Reid is on firmer ground when he thus reduces his hyperbole *re* a "new age." Empirical research [00] confirms his strictures against the sermon as a 'no feedback' situation.

> Harold J. Leavitt and Ronald Mueller set up an experient in which a leader sought to describe a series of geometric patterns to a group of listeners so that the listeners would reproduce the patterns accurately. In one phase of the experiment, the instructor sat behind a partition and was not visible. This was termed "zero feedback": No questions or noises were permitted except by the instructor.'

> The second pattern was labeled the "visible audience" condition. The group members and instructor could see each other, but no speaking was allowed by the members. If they looked puzzled, the instructor was free to "read" this nonverbal communication and modify his message, but they could not speak. The third pattern was one in which the instructor could ask questions to determine if he was being understood, but group members could only reply yes or no. The fourth pattern was a "free feedback" situation. In this case, the group members were allowed to interrupt the instructor, ask questions, and discuss the matter with each other.

> The results of the Leavitt and Mueller studies revealed a steady increase of accuracy as feedback increased. With more feedback, the time required to complete the task also increased. However, an interesting by-product emerged. The researchers noticed that hostility built up in the group members when no feedback was permitted. The hostility was often vented on the leader of the session following the "no feedback" sessions.[34]

Many of us do provide opportunities for sermon "talkback" with some regularity, though unfortunately most of our congregants ordinarily fail to participate. A wise preacher will supplement such talkback with the fullest possible participation in the church's adult education program and in the planning of that programming — to be sure that a variety of voices are heard. (Again, one preaches to edify and to empower a congregation; we "prophesy" only in part. The priestly, administrative, educational and pastoral roles undergird and empower the pulpit in nurturing and being nurtured by "the beloved community of memory and of hope," as Josiah Royce called the church.)

In our time a more or less conventional church service can be a deeply unsettling experience for many who, nevertheless, feel some inchoate need to "keep the sabbath" somehow. In Toledo we "host" an alternative Sunday morning "celebration," held in another part of our building at the same hour as service in the sanctuary. Members of The Fellowship, as this group is called, conduct their own affairs, very much as they please. They share Coffee Hourse with the rest of us; their kids attend our Church School; I do their weddings, etc. The relationship is warm and supportive on both sides. Some Fellowship members do after a time join the congregation in the sanctuary but the opposite happens also — *and that is what makes it so healthy for the church as a whole.* To be a Unitarian Universalist in Toledo you don't have to submit to that man in the pulpit, standing "six feet above contradiction," as the old canard has it! You can choose The Fellowship instead.

The high pulpit and the fixed pews (as in Toledo) are a handicap with which one can learn to live. They are poor symbols of Unitarian Universalism, however, so one a month I bring the children up into the chancel and sit on the floor for dialogue with them, which their parents and other adults enjoy at least as much as they (and I) do. Someday their parents will get the idea that by a few changes in our physical arrangements, we could better symbolize to visitors (and to ourselves) what it is we are trying to do in a Unitarian Universalist church.

As for reaching people "through all the senses at once" (or, to temper Reid's utopianism with a dash of practicality, by more than the preacher's words), many of us are at work on that. We are doing more creative things with music, poetry, dance, and the visual arts. We may even learn the spiritual uses of silence. My old friend, Archie Worthing, would have appreciated Max Picard's thoughts on this subject.

> When language is no longer related to silence, it loses its source of refreshment and renewal and therefore something of its substance. Language today seems to talk automatically, out of

117

its own strength, and, emptying and scattering itself, it seems to be hastening to an end.

There is something hard and obstinate in language today, as though it were making a great effort to remain alive in spite of its emptiness...By taking it away from silence we have made language an orphan. [35]

But in the last analysis I am not convinced that Unitarian Universalists sharing with their preacher the experience of a well-conceived and skillfully executed service and sermon must feel, as Reid suggests, that they are playing the part of "passive spectator" and/or "dependent follower." To listen to a sermon that challenges one's mind is not a "passive-dependent" experience.

I yield the last word to my beloved mentor of forty-five years ago, Dean Sperry. I have found my younger colleagues fulfilling so vibrantly this "Charge to the Preacher," drawn from his Lyman Beecher Lectures:

A minister should be skilled in a knowledge of human nature. He (sic) should be fully a man (sic) and should count nothing human foreign to himself. He should be one who needs not that any testify to him of man, for he knows what is in man. This skill alone might cost a lifetime of discipline. Yet it cannot ever quite be gained by study. It is in equal part of grace which comes to us through a native sympahty and imagination. Without a fellow-feeling for your human kind, no text books in psychology can ever give it to you. The world has a right to expect, when it turns to the minister of religion, that it will meet in him one who understands in advance the secrets which it comes to confess, the perplexities on which it asks advice, the temptations with which it wrestles, the sorrows which burden its heart, the hopes which it can never quite relinquish. What men are, and do, and bear, if not the only study of the minister, is always his proper study. Without an insight into human nautre, compounded of our own first-hand experience of life, of our observation of other men, and of our deepening knowledge of the world's classics, we stand condemned as unskilled workmen in our profession.

A minister should be skilled in ceremonial. The great occasions of life, whether they be private or public, call for recognition and formal expression. To let them pass uncelebrated, or to celebrate them inadequately, is felt to be a grievous error. A marriage performed by a justice of the peace satisfies the requirements of the civil law, but such a ceremony is a meagre symbol of the mysterious transaction in process. The instinct which demands "a church wedding" is more than a desire for the social decencies. The secular prose of things falls short on our major joys and sorrows, our festivals and anniversary times. Man cries out for poetry, and ceremonial is the answer of the race to this cry. Every community needs men who can care for life's proper poetry — what Cardinal Newman once called its "legitimate rhetoric."[36] Needing such men, the community is entitled to persons in whom it can have confidence...

And, finally, our third skill is that of preaching. It is the one by which we shall always be most easily identified and most commonly appraised. I suppose the most familiar judgment passed upon us runs thus: "No, he is not very much of a preacher, but ..he does thus and so pretty well." The initial qualification identifies the yardstick by which we are first measured. The traditional discipline of preaching calls for all the wit and learning and ingenuity we have. Occasionally a sermon can be preached quite extemporaneously. Yet I doubt whether such extemporaneity is as much a thing of the moment as it seems. Behind the power to say things well without immediate preparation lie the years we have spent in giving thought to religion and our discipline in putting words together.

You know, when you hear a man speak, whether there is steady thinking, an independent life of the mind, behind his words. You know whether he has worked patiently and doggedly at the ways of saying things. He cannot deceive you. Whatever else you may think of his sermon — and it does not matter whether you agree with his ideas or not— you respect him as a person fit to live and work in our modern world, if he convinces you that he is a man of discipline and skill. The moral confidence in a preacher's crafts-manship means more to you than agreement with his theology, because his craftsmanship is a clue to his character.[37]

NOTES

INTRODUCTION

1. Wilbur, Earl Morse, *A History of Unitarianism: Socinianism and its Antecedents* (Cambridge: Harvard University Press, 1945), pp. 333-335.
2. Weller, Jack E., Letter, *Christian Century*, February 3-10, 1982, p. 139.
3. Weidman, Judith L., ed., *Women Ministers: How Women are Redefining Traditional Roles* (San Francisco: Harper & Row, 1981). See especially Huie, Janice Riggle, "Preaching Through Metaphor," pp. 49-66.
4. Channing, William Ellery, "Preaching Christ," in *The Works of William E. Channing, D.D.* (Boston: George G. Channing, 1849), Vol. III, pp. 20-22.
5. Channing, William Ellery, "Charge at the Ordination of the Rev. John Sullivan Dwight," in *Ibid.*, Vol. V, pp. 305-306.
6. McFague, Sallie, *Speaking in Parables: A Study in Metaphor and Theology* (Philadelphia: Fortress Press, 1975), p. 62.
7. Shakespeare, William, *Much Ado About Nothing*, Act V, Scene 1, Line 35.
8. Hitchings, Catherine F., *Universalist and Unitarian Women Ministers*, published as Vol. X of *The Journal of the Universalist Historical Society*, p. 45.
9. *Ibid.*, p. 89.
10. Parker, Theodore, "The Transient and the Permanent in Christianity," in Cooke, George Willis, ed., *The Transient and Permanent in Christianity* (Boston: American Unitarian Association, 1908), Centenary Edition, Vol. 4, p. 38.
11. Buechner, Frederick, *The Sacred Journey* (San Francisco: Harper & Row, 1982), p. 69.
12. Parker, Theodore, "Experience as a Minister," in Leighton, Rufus, ed., *Autobiography, Poems and Prayers* (Boston: American Unitarian Association, 1908), Centenary Edition, Vol. 13, pp. 408-409.
13. Romans 10:14-15.

FROM THE MASTHEAD TO THE HATCHES

1. Voss, Carl H., *The Universal God* (Boston: Beacon Press, 1953), p. 76.
2. Locke, Henry Dyer, *An Ancient Parish* (Watertown: First Parish Church, 1930), plate opposite p. 1.
3. de Vries, Peter, *The Mackeral Plaza* (New York: Little, Brown & Company, 1958), p. 188.
4. Miller, Samuel H., "The Mystery of Our Calling," quoted in Mondale, Lester, *Preachers in Purgatory* (Boston: Beacon Press, 1966), p. 30.
5. Matthew 21:22-27.
6. Enslin, Morton, *From Jesus to Christianity* (Boston: Beacon Press, 1964), p. 9.
7. Matthew 5:21.
8. The Acts 9:15.
9. Galatians 1:8-10.
10. Pagels, Elaine, *The Gnostic Gospels* (New York: Vintage Books, 1981), p. 44.
11. Bainton, Roland, *The Reformation of the Sixteenth Century* (Boston: Beacon Press, 1962), p. 11.

12. Luther, Martin, "The Babylonian Captivity of the Church," quoted in *Three Treatises* (Philadelphia. Fortress Press, 1960), p. 217.

13. Bainton, *Op. Cit.*, p. 61.

14. *Ibid.*, p. 129.

15. *Ibid.*, p. 130.

16. Bainton, Roland, *Hunted Heretic,* (Boston: Beacon Press, 1960), pp. 26-27.

17. Bainton, *Reformation*, p. 216.

18. Zweig, Stefan, *The Right to Heresy* (Boston: Beacon Press, 1951), p. 137.

19. Channing, William E. "Demands of the Age on the Ministry," "The Christian Ministry," and "Unitarian Christianity," in *The Works of William E. Channing* (Boston: American Unitarian Association, 1886).

20. Emerson, Ralph Waldo, "The Over-Soul," in *The Selected Writings of Ralph Waldo Emerson* (New York: The Modern Library, 1950), pp. 268-269.

21. Parke, David B., *The Epic of Unitarianism* (Boston: Beacon Press, 1960), p. 111.

22. Küng, Hans, *Does God Exist?* (New York: Vintage Books, 1981), p. 429.

23. *Ibid.*, p. 49.

24. Voss, *Op. Cit.*, p. 84.

PREACHING AS A SACRAMENTAL EVENT

1. The ideas expressed in this section were first introduced in a paper by the author prepared for the Prairie Group, Unitarian Universalist ministers' study group. Delivered in November, 1972, the paper was entitled "A Case for Preaching."

2. Bandler, Richard and Grindler, John, *The Structure of Magic: Language and Therapy* (Palo Alto: Science and Behavior Books, 1975), 2 vols; Bateson, Gregory, *Mind and Nature: A Necessary Unity* (New York: E.P. Dutton, 1979); Bateson, Gregory, *Steps to an Ecology of Mind* (New York: Ballentine Books, 1972); Erickson, Milton H., *Advanced Techniques of Hypnosis and Therapy*, Jay Haley, Editor (New York: Grune and Stratton, 1967); Erickson, Milton H. and Rossi, Ernest L., *Hypnotherapy* (New York: John Wiley and Sons, 1979); Haley, Jay, "Development of a Theory: A History of a Research Project" in *Double Bind: The Foundation of the Communicational Approach to the Family*, Carlos E. Sluzki and Donald C. Ransom, Editors (New York: Grune and Stratton), pp. 59-104; Haley, Jay, *Strategies of Psychotherapy* (New York: Grune and Stratton, 1963); Watzlawick, Paul, et al. *Pragmatics of Human Communication* (New York: W.W. Norton, 1967).

3. Watzlawick, Paul, *The Language of Change* (New York: Basic Books, Inc., 1978), pp. 40-41.

4. *Ibid.*, p. 119.

5. *Op. cit.*, Bandler, pp. 13-14.

6. *Op. cit.*, Watzlawick, p. 46.

7. Diamond, Stuart, *The Double Brain* (Baltimore: Williams and Wilkins, 1972); John C. Eccles, *The Understanding of the Brain* (New York: McGraw-Hill, 1973); Michael S. Gazzaniga, *The Bisected Brain* (New York: Appleton-Century-Crofts, 1970); Marcel Kinsbourne and W. Smith, *Hemispheric Disconnections and Cerebral Function* (Springfield: Charles C. Thomas, 1974); Robert E. Ornstein, *The Psychology of Consciousness* (New York: Penguin, 1977).

8. *Op. cit.*, Watzlawick, p. 47.

9. *The New Yorker*, October 22, 1979, p. 32.

10. *Ibid.*, pp. 32-33.

11. A worthwhile biennial periodical now being published in this field is *The Journal of Mental Imagery*, available through Brandon House, Inc., P.O. Box 240, Bronx, NY 10471.

12. MacLeish, Archibald, *Poetry and Experience* (Baltimore: Penguin, 1964), p. 46.

13. *Ibid.*, p. 69.

14. *Ibid.*, p. 65-66.

15. McFague, Sallie, *Speaking in Parables: A Study in Metaphor and Theology* (Philadelphia: Fortress Press, 1975).

16. Bateson, Gregory, *Mind and Nature: A Necessary Unity* (New York: E.P. Dutton, 1979), p. 218.

17. Forsyth, P.T., *Positive Preaching and the Modern Mind* (London: Independent Press, ca. 1910), p. 57.

18. *Time*, December 31, 1979, p. 64.

19. *Op. cit.*, Forsyth, p. 57.

20. Tillich, Paul, *Systematic Theology* (Chicago: University of Chicago Press, 1963), Vol. III, p. 120.

21. Barth, Karl, source unknown.

MIRRORS NEVER LIE?

1. Urban, W.M. *Language and Reality* (New York: Macmillan, 1939), p. 21.

2. Genesis 1:1-3.

3. John 1:1.

4. Matthew 8:3.

5. II Timothy 4:2.

6. Kiekegaard, Soren, *Repetition* (Princeton: Princeton University Press, 1941), p. 53.

7. II Corinthians 4:5.

8. Quoted in a sermon by the Rev. Robert M. Hemstreet.

9. Kierkegaard, Soren, *Christian Discourses* (London: Oxford University Press, 1940), pp. 206-07.

10. Channing, William Ellery, "Charge at the Ordination of the Rev. John Sullivan Dwight," in *The Works of William E. Channing, D.D.* (Boston: George G. Channing, 1849), Vol. V, p. 306.

11. Rich, Adrienne, *Dream of a Common Language* (New York: Norton, 1978), p. 67

12. I am indebted to the Rev. Linnea Pearson for this insight, articulated by her in the Charge to the Minister at the Installation of the Rev. Daniel Hotchkiss, Boca Raton, FL, 1981.

13. Heidegger, Martin, *Being and Time* (New York: Harper & Row, 1962).

14. Isaiah 61:1-2.

15. Quoted in a sermon by the Rev. David C. Pohl.

16. Many of the ideas in this essay were developed many years ago in conversation with the Rev. R. Lanier Clance, minister of the First Extentialist Church of Atlanta. Though

responsibility for their formulation here is entirely mine, I am grateful for these conversations which shaped my own practice of preaching in many significant ways.

THE WIZARDRY OF WORDS

1. Tapp, Robert B., *Religion Among the Unitarian Universalists* (New York: Seminar Press, 1973, p. 80.
2. See Fowler, James and Keen, Sam, in Beryman, Jerome, ed., *Life Maps: Conversations on the Journey of Faith* (Minneapolis: Winston Press and Waco, Tx: Word Books, 1978).
3. Phillips, Roy, "Preaching as a Sacramental Event" (see pp. 00).
4. Nichols, J. Randall, *Building the Word* (San Francisco: Harper & Row, 1980).
5. *Ibid*., p. 71.
6. *Op. Cit.*, Phillips.
7. Cameron-Bandler, Leslie, *They Lived Happily Ever After: Methods for Achieving Happy Endings in Coupling* (Cupertino, CA: Meta Publications, 1978).
8. Buechner, Frederick, *Telling the Truth: The Gospel as Tragedy, Comedy and Fairy Tale* (San Francisco: Harper & Row, 1977), p. 98.

THE PREACHER AS PROPHET

1. Adams, James Luther, *On Being Human Religiously* (Boston: Beacon Press, 1976), p. 137.
2. von Rad, Gerhard, *The Message of the Prophets* (New York: Harper & Row, 1967), p. 13.
3. *Ibid*., pp. 113 ff.
4. *Ibid*.
5. Goldberg, David, *Meet the Prophets* (New York: Bookman Associates, 1956), p. 31. Goldberg is one of many scholars to use this term. See also Anderson, Bernard, *Understanding the Old Testament* (Prentice Hall, 1966), pp. 189 ff.; and Wright, G. Ernest & Fuller, R. H., *The Book of the Acts of God* (Garden City, N.Y.: Doubleday Anchor, 1960, p. 149 ff.
6. Trible, Phyllis, "Depatriarchalizing in Biblical Interpretation," *Journal of the American Academy of Religion*, Vol XLI, No. 1 (March 1973), pp. 30-48. For further refinement and amplification of this principle, see "Feminist Hermeneutics and Biblical Studies" by the same author in *The Christian Century* (February 3-10, 1982), pp. 116-8. Also her book, *God and the Rhetoric of Sexuality*, (Philadephia, 1978).
7. For a comprehensive listing of feminine references in the Bible, see *Biblical Affirmations of Woman* by Leonard Swindler,(Westminster Press, 1979). Mr. Swindler is Professor of Interreligious Dialogue and Catholic Studies at Temple University.
8. Wright, G. Ernest and Fuller, Reginald H., *The Book of the Acts of God: Contemporary Scholarship Interprets the Bible* (Garden City, NY: Doubleday Anchor, 1976), p. 150.
9. Adams, James Luther, *Taking Time Seriously* (Glencoe, IL: The Free Press, 1957), pp. 42-58. Also found in *Op. cit.*, Adams, pp. 102-119.
10. *Op. cit.*, von Rad, p. 100.
11. Adams, James Luther, "Theological Bases of Social Action," in *Op. Cit.*, Adams, *Taking Time*, p. 51.

12. Ruether, Rosemary Radford, *Disputed Questions: On Being a Christian* (Nashville: Abingdon Press, 1982), p.101.

13. *Op. cit.*, Wright and Fuller, p. 151.

14. *Op. cit.*, von Rad, pp. 230-231

15. Freire, Paulo, *Pedagogy of the Oppressed* (New York: Seabury Press, 1970), p. 129.

16. Burghardt, Walter J., S. J., *Tell the Next Generation: Homilies and Near Homilies* (New York: Paulist Press, 1980), p. 10.

17. Armstrong, James, *Telling Truth: The Foolishness of Preaching in a Real World* (Waco, TX: Word Books, 1977), p. 15.

THE EMPOWERING SERMON

1. Melville, Herman, *Moby Dick* (New York, 1950), p.50.

2. Baxter, Batsell Barrett, *The Heart of the Yale Lectures* (New York, 1947), pp. 5, 123.

3. *Time*, December 31, 1979, p.64.

4. Cited by Becker, Edwin L., "Role of the Minister in Contemporary Culture," *The Drake University Bulletin on Religion,* Vol. xvi, (November, 1953), p.3

5. *New England's First Fruits* , 1643. These words appear on the Harvard College gates.

6. Statistics and chronology from Morris, Richard B., *Encyclopedia of American History* (New York, 1953).

7. Stephen, Sir Leslie, *Hours in a Library* (New York, 1904) Vol II, Ch. 2, "Jonathan Edwards."

8. Cited by Sidney Mead in his chapter in Niebuhr, H. Richard and Williams, Daniel D., eds , *The Ministry in Historical Perspectives* (New York, 1956), p 239 This work consists of a series of historical essays commissioned by the Study of Theological Education in the United States and Canada as background for the Study. The essays cover the entire period of Christian history. Major emphasis is given to preaching and within these pages the reader will find the best short treatment of the history of sermonizing in Europe and America. Unitarian Universalists should take some pride in noting that three of the six scholars selected for the project are from our fellowship: Dr. Mead, Dr. George Huntston Williams and Dr. Roland Bainton.

9. *Ibid.*, pp. 235-36.

10. *Ibid.*, p. 244.

11. John Burroughs, cited by Thompson, Ernest Tirce, *Changing Emphases in American Preaching* (Philadelphia, 1943), p. 75.

12. Drummond, Andrew Landale, *Story of American Protestanism* (Boston, 1950), p. 375.

13. Citations found in Baxter, *op. cit.*, pp. 5, 123.

14. See Wright, Conrad, "Salute the Arriving Moment," chapter 3 of C. Wright, ed., *A Stream of Light* (Boston, 1975).

15. Cited by Ahlstrom, Sydney E., in "The Middle Period, 1840-1880," *The Harvard Divinity School,* George Huntston Williams, ed. (Boston, 1954), p. 120.

16. Frost, S.E., Jr., *The World's Great Sermons* (New York, 1943), p. 227. Doan began his career as a teacher of psychology and education but turned to teaching theology and was ordained a Unitarian minister in 1914.

17. *Ibid.*, p. 220.

18. *Ibid.*, p. 350.

19. *Ibid.*, pp. 329-30.

20. From a tape of Dr. Frederick May Eliot.

21. From a tape of the sermon supplied by Dr. Donald Harrington.

22. From a tape available from The Foundation for Christian Living, Pawling, New York. "I" and "my" occur 27 times in this 3.5 minute segment as compared with 10 minutes in Holmes' 57 seconds of tape.

23. From a recording, *The Voice of A. Powell Davies, Vol. 1,* available from Publications Committee, All Souls Unitarian Church, Washington, DC. Those pronouns ("I" — "my") are heard six times in 3.75 minutes.

24. From tape supplied by St. Agnes Church. Sheen uses "I" and "my" (referring to himself) 24 times in 5 minutes and 55 seconds.

25. In his last thirteen years Davies' preaching was addressed to sophisticated minds in that U.S. metropolitan area then functioning as the most powerful magnet to draw such minds together into one place in the land. His is not a model to be followed in East Greenwich, RI or Sioux City, IA. And Davies "got away with" speaking fast and using a vocabulary unfamiliar even to some of his congregation because in his last years he had become a "cult figure" and thus the beneficiary of privileges of expression allowed few of the rest of us.

26. Donald McLeod, professor of preaching and worship at Princeton Theological Seminary, says ". . . In the seminary where I teach, sermons preached by the women excel to a conspicuous degree. . . ." *Christian Century,* Feb. 1-8, 1982, p. 100.

27. *Ibid.*, p. 98. Dr. McLeod says much the same thing about his students' sermons. "As a teacher of preachers for 30 years, I have never heard such consistently good preaching as today. This augurs well for the future. I, for one, am filled with hope."

28. Sperry, Willard L., *We Prophesy in Part* (New York & London, 1938), p. 114.

29. *Ibid.*, pp. 131-3. Above, in categories 10 through 13 of my listing of the subject matter of the seventy-two contemporary sermons I have read for this paper, I have meant to suggest that thirty-one of them dealt with what Sperry here refers to as "these deep, constant, recurring concerns."

30. Reid, Clyde, *The Empty Pulpit* (New York, Evanston, and London, 1967), p. 60.

31. *Ibid.*, p. 61. I'm sure Jerry Falwell agrees.

32. *Ibid.*, p. 60-61.

33. Leavitt, Harold J. and Mueller, Ronald A.H., "Some Effects of Feedback on Communication," *Human Relations,* IV (Spring, 1951), pp. 401-410.

34. *Op. cit.*, Reid, pp. 79-80.

35. Picard, Max, in Godman, Stanley, trans., *The World of Silence* (Chicago, 1952), p. 41.

36. I did my last year at Harvard Divinity School with Sperry, working with him on a book on the Christian mystics (*Strangers and Pilgrims,* Boston, 1939), several of the best of them women. Sperry is using the language of 1938 here. Having known him well, I am sure he would now say, "Every community needs today men *and women.* . . ." Edit this quotation to eliminate its sexist language and then cherish its wisdom!

Sperry's wife, Muriel, dropped him off at his Congregational Church when, in earlier years, he was a pastor; then she drove off to the Episcopal Church she regularly attended. Sperry's congregation rarely saw her except thus, at the wheel of the family car. A parson who cherished a wife who thus lived her own life in the earliest years of this century is not to be judged chauvinistic.

37. Sperry, *Op. cit.*, pp. 157-161. *We Prophesy in Part,* written in 1938, contains some "dated" lines, but is still, in my judgment, the best treatise on preaching presently avaialble. Sperry's *Reality in Worship* (New York, 1925) is an equally valuable manual on the work of the preacher in the conduct of worship.

SELECTED BIBLIOGRAPHY

Armstrong, James, *Telling Truth: The Foolishness of Preaching in the Real World*, 1977. Word Books, Waco, Texas. This book and Burghardt's book, *Tell the Next Generation*, are two books on contemporary preaching from master preachers. James Armstrong is a Methodist Bishop with a strong emphasis on the prophetic dimension of preaching.

Buechner, Frederick, *Telling the Truth: The Gospel as Tragedy, Comedy and Fairy Tale* 1977, Harper and Row, San Francisco.

Burghardt, Walter J., S. J., *Telling the Next Generation: Homilies and Near Homilies*, 1980, Paulist Press, N.Y. This book and James Armstrong's *Telling Truth* are two books on contemporary preaching from master preachers. Walter Burghardt is a Jesuit theologian.

Channing, William Ellery, *Charge for the Ordination of Rev. Robert C. Waterston*, in *Works* (Vol. V), 1849 edition, see especially pp. 287-291.

Channing, William Ellery, *Charge at the Ordination of Rev. John Sullivan Dwight*, in *Works* (Vol. V), 1849 edition see especially pp. 305-312. Excellent statements of balance between reflection and emotion in the sermonic presentation.

Claypool, John R., *The Preaching Event*, 1980, Word Publishers, Waco, TX. The 1979 Lyman Beecher Lectures on preaching delivered at Yale University. Simple points put well.

Cox, James W., *Biblical Preaching*, 1983, Westminster Press, Philadelphia.

Craddock, Fred, *Overhearing the Gospel*, 1978, Abingdon Press, Nashville, TN.

Crocker, Lionel, *Harry Emerson Fosdick's Art of Preaching*, 1971, Charles C. Thomas: Springfield, IL. Collection of seven essays by Fosdick on preaching and fourteen commentaries on Fosdick's own preaching.

Huie, Janice Riggle, *Preaching Through Metaphor*, in Weidman, Judith L., ed., *Women Ministers*, 1981, Harper and Row, San Francisco.

Mitchell, Henry H., *The Recovery of Preaching*, 1977, Harper and Row, San Francisco. Reflections based upon the black preaching tradition but applicable to all traditions with special attention to the use of personal experience, story telling, and dialogues.

Nichols, J. Randall, *Building the Word*, 1980, Harper and Row: San Francisco, particularly Chapters 11 and 12.

Nouwen, Henri J.M., *The Wounded Healer: Ministry in Contemporary Society*, 1972, Doubleday & Co., Garden City. A "classic" in the field of ministry arts; the basis for much of the theory expounded by Claypool and others.

Sperry, Willard L., *Reality In Worship*, 1925, Macmillan, New York.

Sperry, Willard L., *We Prophesy In Part*, 1938, Harper & Bros., New York.

(The following three books are for background in the feminist hermeneutic in using biblical references:)

Trible, Phyllis, *God and the Rhetoric of Sexuality*, 1978, Fortress Press, Philadelphia.

Trible, Phyllis, "Feminist Hernemeutics and Biblical Studies," *The Christian Century*, February 3-10, 1982; pp. 116-8.

Trible, Phyllis, "Depatriarchalizing in Biblical Interpretation," *Journal of the America Academy of Religion*, Vol. XLI, No. 1 (March 1973), pp. 30-48.

VonRad, Gerhard, *The Message of the Prophets*, 1967, Harper and Row paperback, NY. Excellent reference work on the latest scholarship on the classical prophets of Israel; provocative for prophetic preaching today.

Wardlaw, Don M. (editor), *Preaching Biblically*, 1983, Westminster Press, Philadelphia.

Spinning a Sacred Yarn: Women Speak from the Pulpit, 1982, the Pilgrim Press: NY. A collection of sermons preached by women from both the Christian and Jewish traditions.

THE CONTRIBUTORS

JUDITH L. HOEHLER, a graduate of Harvard Divinity School, is Minister of the First Parish in Weston, Massachusetts. She and her husband, Harry, were one of the first "clergy couples" in the Unitarian Universalist movement. She is a member of the Board of Overseers of Bowdoin College, Brunswick, Maine.

IRVING R. MURRAY is Minister of the First Unitarian Church of Toledo, Ohio, a position he assumed in 1977 after ministries in Pittsburgh, Baltimore and Garden City, Long Island. Irving is a jazz enthusiast and an accomplished jazz pianist.

ROY D. PHILLIPS has for the past twelve years been Minister of Unity Church, St. Paul, Minnesota. Roy is a graduate of Meadville/Lombard Theological School in Chicago and served the Unitarian Universalist Church of Racine, Wisconsin, before going to St. Paul.

DAVID O. RANKIN is Minister of the Fountain Street Church in Grand Rapids, Michigan, a congregation which is not affiliated with a larger denominational body. He has served Unitarian Universalist churches in Watertown and New Bedford, Massachusetts, San Francisco and Atlanta, and is the author of a collection of sermons entitled *So Great a Cloud of Witnesses*, published in 1978 by Strawberry Hill Press.

WILLIAM F. SCHULZ is Executive Vice President of the Unitarian Universalist Association, having previously served the Association as Director of Social Responsibility. He was Minister of the First Parish in Bedford, Massachusetts (Unitarian Universalist) from 1975 to 1978.

JOYCE H. SMITH is Director of the Department of Ministerial and Congregational Services of the Unitarian Universalist Association. She has served churches in Sherborn, Massachusetts, and Bethesda, Maryland. Joyce likes occasionally to try her hand at poetry.

INDEX